Great Meals in Minutes was created by Rebus, Inc. and published by Time-Life Books.

Rebus, Inc.

Publisher: Rodney Friedman
Editor: Shirley Tomkievicz
Art Director: Ronald Gross
Senior Editors: Brenda Goldberg, Ruth A. Peltason
Food Editor and Food Stylist: Grace Young
Photographer: Steven Mays
Prop Stylist: Zazel Wilde Lovén
Staff Writer: Alexandra Greeley
Production Manager: Peter Sparber
Editorial Assistants: Jennifer Mah, Teri Tolen, Michael Flint
Photography, Styling Assistant: Cathryn Schwing
Editorial Board: Angelica Cannon, Sally Dorst, Lilyan Glusker, Kim MacArthur, Valerie Marchant, Joan Whitman

For information about any Time-Life book, please write:
Reader Information
Time-Life Books
541 North Fairbanks Court
Chicago, Illinois 60611

Library of Congress Cataloging in Publication Data
Chinese menus.
   (Great meals in minutes)
   Includes index.
   1. Cookery, Chinese. 2. Cooks—Biography.
I. Time-Life Books. II. Series.
TX724.5.C5C56144 1983   642   83-5118
ISBN 0-86706-159-6 (lib. bdg.)
ISBN 0-86706-158-8 (retail ed.)

Time-Life Books Inc. is a wholly owned subsidiary of

Time Incorporated

Founder: Henry R. Luce 1898-1967
Editor-in-Chief: Henry Anatole Grunwald
President: J. Richard Munro
Chairman of the Board: Ralph P. Davidson
Executive Vice President: Clifford J. Grum
Editorial Director: Ralph Graves
Group Vice President, Books: Joan D. Manley

SERIES CONSULTANT
Margaret E. Happel is the author of *Ladies Home Journal Adventures in Cooking*, *Ladies Home Journal Handbook of Holiday Cuisine*, and other best-selling cookbooks, as well as the translator and adapter of Rebecca Hsu Hiu Min's *Delights of Chinese Cooking*. A food consultant based in New York City, she has been director of the food department of *Good Housekeeping* and editor of *American Home* magazine.

WINE CONSULTANT
Tom Maresca combines a full-time career teaching English literature with writing about and consuming fine wines. He is now at work on *The Wine Case Book*, which explains the techniques of wine tasting.

Cover: Mai Leung's spinach and egg shred soup, diced chicken, Szechwan style, and stir-fried green beans with garlic. See pages 96–97.

$6—
P&A
CB

Great Meals
IN MINUTES
CHINESE
MENUS

TIME-LIFE BOOKS, ALEXANDRIA, VIRGINIA

Contents

Meet the Cooks

JEAN YUEH

Lecturer, TV guest chef, and food consultant Jean Yueh has taught Chinese cooking for more than fifteen years. Her books include *The Great Tastes of Chinese Cooking—Contemporary Methods and Menus* (retitled, in paperback, *Great Chinese Cooking—From Fire Pot to Food Processor*), which won the R. T. French Tastemaker Award in 1980 as the best Oriental cookbook, and *Dim Sum and Chinese One-Dish Meals.*

BARBARA TROPP

Barbara Tropp is a retired scholar turned Chinese cook. After studying Chinese art and literature at Princeton University, she lived for two years in Taiwan, where she learned to appreciate Chinese cooking. She returned home to New Jersey and became a practitioner and teacher of the art. She is the author of the highly acclaimed *The Modern Art of Chinese Cooking.* She is now preparing to open her own restaurant, China Moon, in San Francisco.

AUDREY AND CALVIN LEE

The late Calvin Lee came from a long line of professional chefs, starting his cooking career at age 17 in his family's New York restaurant. A lawyer and businessman as well, he was also a college president. Audrey Lee, born in Philadelphia and now living in Chatham, New Jersey, learned Chinese cooking from her husband. Together, they wrote several cookbooks, including *The Gourmet Chinese Regional Cookbook, Chinese Cooking for American Kitchens,* and *Chinatown, U.S.A.*

NINA SIMONDS

Nina Simonds, author of *Classic Chinese Cuisine,* has translated and edited several other books, including *Chinese Cuisine* and *Chinese Snacks.* She learned to cook in Taiwan under the direction of Chinese master chef Huang Su-Huei. She also studied for a year at La Varenne Ecole de Cuisine in Paris and is the holder of a Grande Diplome in classic French cooking. Her articles have appeared in *Gourmet* and *Cuisine* magazines, and she is a regular contributor to *The Boston Globe.*

MICHAEL TONG

A Shanghai native brought up in Taiwan and Hong Kong, Michael Tong is a restaurateur whose personal hobby also is cooking. He came to the United States in 1963 and then settled in New York in 1966. He owns and directs the three Shun Lee restaurants in Manhattan, as well as one of the first restaurants in this country to feature the spicy cooking of Hunan.

JERI SIPE

Jeri Sipe was born in Taiwan, the daughter of impoverished farmers, and learned to cook before she learned to read. By the age of nine, she was working as a cook in a wealthy household, and by adulthood, she had become a full-fledged, if largely self-taught, professional. She now lives on a farm near Portland, Oregon, with her American husband and three children, and since 1971 has taught cooking classes in Portland.

KEN HOM

Author and cooking teacher Ken Hom, who now lives in Berkeley, California, began to cook at age eleven in his uncle's Chinese restaurant in Chicago. This well-known cooking teacher often guides culinary tours to Hong Kong and has a cooking school there as well. Ken Hom, author of *Chinese Techniques*, is doing a series on Chinese cooking for the BBC, to be aired in 1984, and is also publishing two books the same year.

KAREN LEE

Karen Lee, a New Yorker, has traveled to China to collect Chinese recipes. A cooking teacher and caterer for the past twelve years, she is the author of *Chinese Cooking for the American Kitchen* and *Chinese Cooking Secrets*. She has recently introduced a line of Chinese sauces and condiments that is being sold through specialty food shops.

MAI LEUNG

Mai Leung was born in Canton and raised in Canton and Hong Kong. She learned to cook while still at home, then later studied in Hong Kong with chefs from various regions of China. To enhance her knowledge of other regional cuisines, she traveled through China and Taiwan. She began her teaching career in Chicago and later taught in the New York–New Jersey area. She is the author of *The Classic Chinese Cook Book* and *Mai Leung's Dim Sum and Other Chinese Street Food*.

Chinese Menus in Minutes

Thousands of years before Americans turned fast food into a national passion, Chinese cooks had mastered the art of preparing great meals quickly—and easily. Their invention was born of necessity. The family kitchen usually consisted of nothing more than a small container of coals. Fuel was scarce, and because there often was not enough land or grain to bring crops to maturity, so was food. The Chinese learned that young, tender vegetables and meats sliced, diced, minced, or shredded were easy to share. They also cooked faster than big pieces and, therefore, required less cooking fuel. The family chef working over the fire needed only a chopping surface, a sharp knife, a pan, and a pair of chopsticks for stirring.

For today's cook, with little time to spend in the kitchen, the Chinese way with food is still one of the fastest and most economical for delicious, nourishing family meals as well as for memorable company dinners.

Furthermore, these time-proven techniques produce better-tasting, fresher foods than do many of the slower Western methods. Everything comes to the table bite-sized: nobody has to carve. And the shreds, slices, and dices look as good as they taste—particularly the vegetables, which hold their bright colors and their vitamins much better when cooked the Chinese way.

Best of all, Chinese cooking is not a mysterious art that takes years to master. The skills of the Chinese kitchen are as easy to acquire as they are invaluable to the good cook in a hurry. Like any other type of cuisine, the Chinese has its ground rules, which are easy to assimilate because, delightfully enough, they make good sense.

On the following pages, nine of America's most talented Chinese cooks present twenty-seven complete menus, all of them within reach of even a beginner. Each meal will serve four people, and the whole menu is cookable in an hour or less. Most, but not all, of the cooks focus on the classic Chinese stir-fry technique, which means rapid cooking in small amounts of oil over high heat. The recipes represent China's fascinating variety of regional styles, from Peking to Canton. Though each recipe is adapted to

A whole fish, some fresh shrimp, and slices of beef, opposite, are ready for cooking Chinese style. On the countertop as well are vegetables and seasonings characteristic of Chinese cooking (clockwise from top left): chilies, Chinese black mushrooms, baby corn, snow peas, fresh ginger, scallions, Oriental eggplants, bok choy, coriander, salted black beans, tree ear mushrooms, whole water chestnuts, and white radishes.

the American supermarket and kitchen, none of them contains any unauthentic shortcuts or any ingredients that would be out of place in the best Chinese kitchens.

The cooks have created these original meals to provide pleasing contrasts not only in taste but also in texture and color. The color photographs accompanying each meal show exactly how the dishes will look when you take them to the table. The table settings, which you can follow or vary as you choose, feature bright colors, simple flower arrangements, and attractive, if not necessarily expensive, serving pieces. You may also wish to add a few Oriental utensils to your own tableware supply: chopsticks with chopstick rests, rice bowls, a teapot and small tea cups without handles, and small sauce bowls for passing at the table.

With the advice of the cooks, the editors suggest for each menu the most compatible teas, wines, and other beverages as well as quick and easy desserts that you may want to serve with the meals. On each recipe page, too, you will find a range of other tips. All the recipes have been meticulously tested for both taste and appearance and to make sure that even a relatively inexperienced cook can do them within the time limit.

If you are trying Chinese cooking for the first time, you may be surprised to find that the main elements are decidedly not exotic. The fact is, virtually all kinds of good food are a part of Chinese cuisine, and you will find comparatively few unfamiliar items in these menus. Indeed, many of the recipes can be prepared from ingredients that are already on your pantry shelves or available in any grocery store. For example, Jean Yueh's Lemon Chicken with Stir-Fried Zucchini and Carrots (page 23) uses ingredients commonly found in an American kitchen.

For some of the other menus, you will, of course, need special spices, sauces, and a few canned goods, as specified in the pantry list on pages 14 and 15. Most of them are in your local supermarket. Many markets now stock a whole Chinese shelf and sell such Oriental staples as mung bean sprouts, fresh ginger, and bok choy (Chinese cabbage) in the produce section. If your hometown has a Chinese population of any size, you will probably find a specialty shop that offers *hoisin* sauce, canned baby corn, water chestnut powder, and Chinese dried mushrooms. And if you cannot find such a shop, see page 103 for a list of dealers who will mail whatever you need. The cooks have also tried to ease your way by telling you when you can use substitutes without sacrificing the quality of your meal.

BEFORE YOU START

This book will work best when you follow these suggestions:

1. Be organized. Start by taking a few minutes to study the cooking techniques on the following pages and refer back to them when you need to. They will quickly become second nature and will help you turn out professional Chinese meals in minutes. Check the pantry and utensil lists, too, that begin on page 14. You cannot cook quickly without the proper tools and ingredients on hand.

2. Read the menus before you shop. Each one opens with a list of all the required ingredients and provides you with a ready-made shopping list for the things that are not already in your pantry or refrigerator. Be sure, too, to follow the step-by-step game plan for each menu.

3. Remember that the preparation of ingredients for a Chinese meal takes longer than the actual cooking. Although each meal in this volume takes only an hour to prepare, you can, if you like, do the chopping and slicing earlier in the day and then spend only moments at the stove for the final cooking.

4. Study the recipes for each menu carefully. Then make the rounds of the refrigerator, spice shelves, and pantry to assemble your ingredients and tools. When you start the preparatory work—peeling, chopping, mincing—finish *all* before you begin cooking. This is important because you will not have time to stop in the middle of a stir fry to chop up vegetables or meats or to search for a missing sauce. Organizing everything and assembling ingredients ahead of time will insure efficient cooking.

5. Do as the professional cooks do. Put all your ingredients in separate piles on a tray or cutting board, grouping the piles according to the recipe you are preparing. Another good idea is to use separate paper plates and cups for each of the various raw ingredients. You can even number each plate in the order you need it and then easily transfer the food to the pan.

6. Think small. You will notice that most of the recipes in this book call for cooking only a pound or so of meat at a time. This is because Chinese techniques are not designed for large portions: if you try to stir fry too much at a time, the oil will cook off, and the food will not brown properly. Nor can you steam a large amount of food successfully; it will cook too slowly and get watery.

7. When you want to make a bigger meal, prepare additional recipes rather than double quantities. If you are serving six, add one dish to the menu, and two extra dishes for eight. If you do decide to double a dish, cook it in two batches.

A NOTE ON REGIONAL STYLES

China, with a climate that varies from sub-Arctic to tropical, produces an enormous variety of food for the largest and most diverse population in the world. Not surprisingly, cooking styles and preferences vary from one end of the land to the other and from one city to another. Many of the recipes in this volume are southern Chinese, others come from the North, East, and West. Here is a brief guide to regional styles and names:

Eastern China
The seaport of Shanghai, where the Yangstze River empties into the East China Sea, is prominent in this region. The cuisine of the whole area often goes by the name Shanghai. Rice, fish, pork, and beef are basic here: Shanghai cooks tend to braise meats, that is, to simmer them gently in a liquid comprised of soy sauce, sugar, and spices. This technique, known as "red-cooking," is a hallmark of the Shanghai cooking style. Calvin and Audrey Lee's recipe for Lion's Head (meatballs simmered in a seasoned broth) on page 43 is one example of this style.

Northern China
Peking—for centuries the political, cultural, and culinary center of China—still remains the dominant influence in the North. However, the northern provinces of Hunan, Shantung, and Shensi also have their distinct specialties.

The frigid climate of the northern plains makes rice cultivation impossible. Instead, wheat is the staple crop, and wheat-based products, such as noodles, dumplings, and pancakes, are the basis of northern cooking. The more sophisticated cooking style of the North is likely to feature extravagant amounts of rice wine in sauces and marinades. The area is famous for lamb as well as for lots of onion and garlic. Nina Simonds' Drunken Mushrooms on page 51 is an example of northern Chinese cooking, as is Calvin and Audrey Lee's Shantung Chicken with Hot Hoisin Sauce, page 41.

Western China
Szechwan and Hunan—which Americans usually (and rightly) associate with beef dishes and peppery sauces—are the best known provincial cuisines in the West. Western Chinese cooks, indeed, are fond of spices, particularly chili peppers with an almost legendary fire. Barbara Tropp's Spicy Hunan Beef and Hot and Sour Hunan Carrots, page 28, represent that province, while Ken Hom's Stir-Fried Squash, page 79, and Mai Leung's Diced Chicken, page 97, are typical Szechwan dishes.

Southern China
Canton and British-ruled Hong Kong, which is at the tip of mainland China, dominate the South, where rice, fish, pork, and fresh vegetables are staples and the emphasis is generally on minimal cooking time. Cantonese cooks favor crisp, fresh ingredients seasoned with delicate spices and flavorings, so that southern cooking is subtle rather than fiery. Oyster sauce and sweet-and-sour dishes flavored with fresh ginger and soy sauce are Cantonese specialties. Mai Leung's Beef and Scallops with Oyster Sauce, page 102, and Jean Yueh's Lemon Chicken, page 23, are both Cantonese dishes.

PREPARING THE INGREDIENTS

Since much of the food for these Chinese menus must be cut into small pieces before cooking, your most basic tools are a convenient cutting surface and a sharp knife or, if you prefer, a Chinese cleaver. A food processor is not an absolute necessity, but it is a great time-saver. However, even the best processor cannot replace the cutting board and knife: roll cutting, for example, must be done by hand. Besides, most practiced cooks enjoy doing some of their own chopping and dicing whether or not they own a processor.

The best cutting surface is a lightweight hardwood board, lightweight because you will often want to lift and tilt it to scrape the food onto a dish or into the cooking pan. Wooden boards should be washed down in boiling water after preparing meat, poultry, or fish on them. A rectangle of acrylic can also serve as a very good cutting surface. Material harder than wood or acrylic will blunt your knife—the cook's most valued possession.

For your basic chopping knife, choose one with a 10-inch blade, a good multipurpose size. You will also need a smaller paring knife. There are now available many good-quality stainless steel knives designed for professional cooking, and they are easy to care for. Although carbon steel takes a sharp edge, it tends to rust: you must wash and dry it after each use, or it will blacken. Moreover, it is difficult to find carbon steel knives. Never put a fine knife in the dishwasher. Rinse it, dry it, and put it away after use. The equipment section, pages 16 and 17, tells more about caring for knives and cleavers.

Precision cutting is fundamental to Chinese cooking. Food must be both uniformly and beautifully cut for even, quick cooking and for artistic presentation. To satisfy these needs, the Chinese have designed a versatile 3-way tool—the cleaver—which has a razor-sharp edge for cutting, a blunt top edge for pounding, and two broad sides for flattening and scooping up food pieces.

A traditional Chinese cook owns at least three basic cleavers. The largest and heaviest is designed for rugged chopping and is sturdy enough to split through beef and pork bones. This cleaver weighs about 1¾ pounds and has an 8- to 9-inch blade. The medium-weight cleaver is designed especially for cutting, slitting, and jointing poultry. This knife weighs about 1½ pounds and has a 9-inch blade. The lightweight cleaver is ideal for slicing vegetables and boned meats. It weighs about ¾ of a pound and has an 8-inch-long blade. For Western cooks, who may ask their butcher or meatman to chop through bones, the lightweight vegetable cleaver of high-quality stainless steel is the most practical of the three. But a hefty Western knife can do many of the same chores.

Cutting Techniques

The techniques for cutting described below all require a little practice before you can do them quickly. Two basic tips: to cut anything fast and uniformly you must keep it steady on the cutting board. Carrots, garlic, onions, and other round vegetables will roll. Therefore, except when you are roll cutting, start by slicing them in half lengthwise or crosswise to create a flat surface. Then put the flat surface downward and finish the work. Meats cut more easily when they are cold. Try chilling meat for half an hour in the freezer before you dice it, but take it out before it freezes.

Slicing: The simplest way of cutting. Place the food on the board. Hold it firmly with the fingertips of one hand,

which should be close to the cutting edge, with your fingernails toward the knife blade. Your fingertips should be curved under, so that you cannot accidentally cut yourself. Using an easy back-and-forth motion, but not a strenuous sawing motion, with just the weight of the knife and your hand for pressure, cut off pieces in even strips, according to recipe specifications. By keeping your knife razor-sharp, you will need very little muscle power to do this.

Dicing: Cutting food into small squares. Begin by slicing. Then, while holding the slices together in a stack, slice again, leaving about ¼ to ½ inch between cuts. Finally, turn the food or the cutting board a half turn and slice once more at ¼- to ½-inch intervals. For a fine dice, begin by cutting the food in half horizontally. Keep it stacked, then slice it two more times.

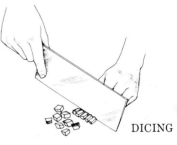

DICING

Mincing: Dicing carried a step further to produce the smallest possible pieces. Proceed with dicing as in the diagram. Then, using the blade of your knife or cleaver, push the pieces into a tight pile. With your cutting hand, grasp the knife by the handle and take the pointed end between the thumb and forefinger of your hand. Hold down the pointed end firmly on the cutting board and, using quick, vertical motions of the handle, chop across the pile in one direction and then the other, pausing now and then to push the pieces into a pile again. If you are using a cleaver, grasp the handle only and keep remaking the pile with the blade. The process may go slowly at first, but with practice you should be able to mince an onion in 60 seconds.

Julienne: A matchstick cut for firm-textured vegetables such as carrots or potatoes and for cooked meats such as ham. For the first step, proceed as though you were dicing. But after stacking your slices, instead of cutting the food into small squares, slice the stack into long, thin pieces about the size and shape of a wooden kitchen match.

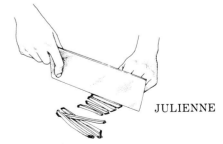

JULIENNE

Shredding: Creating long, thin pieces similar to the julienne but much finer. Do everything as in julienne. Then, holding the knife tip on the board with one hand and the handle in the other, keep cutting lengthwise through the pieces until they are as fine as you can make them. Though an experienced cook can shred with a knife, a hand grater or food processor will do the job faster. Note: if you are shredding vegetables or meats in a food processor, proceed with care. A few seconds' overprocessing will turn a shred into a puree.

Roll cutting: A special method for long cylindrical vegetables such as carrots, asparagus, or zucchini. First, peel the vegetable if the recipe so directs. Now make a sharp, diagonal cut perhaps an inch from one end and try for about a 45-degree angle. Then roll the vegetable a quarter turn and slice again at the same angle, about an inch from the first cut. Continue until you have sliced the whole length. Because the diagonal slices expose more of the insides of the vegetables, they will cook faster and absorb more flavor than will conventional slices.

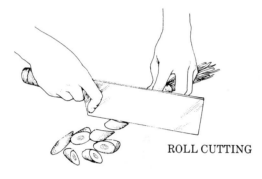

ROLL CUTTING

COOKING TECHNIQUES
Cooking with Oil: Stir Frying

A basic technique of Chinese cooking is stir frying: quickly cooking small amounts of bite-sized chopped foods in small amounts of oil over high heat. The purpose of stir frying is to cook food until just done—never to overcook it—and to infuse it with seasonings. In order to do this, you first add the seasonings (garlic, herbs, spices) to the hot oil, which causes the fragrance and flavor almost literally to explode. Then you add the food, sliced, chopped, diced, or minced uniformly. To keep the food from scorching, you must keep it in motion both by shaking the pan slightly and by stirring it, either with a pair of 16-inch chopsticks, a wooden or metal spatula, or a long-handled spoon. Because the oil must be very hot but not smoking, part of the technique is to adjust the heat up and down from time to time so that the temperature of the oil remains constant.

To stir fry successfully, therefore, you need a heavy-bottomed metal pan with sloping sides designed for even conduction of heat and with a handle or handles that allow you to move it over the heat source. The interior surface must be smooth so that food does not stick to it and burn, and so that you can cook successive batches without stopping to wash the pot.

You should choose one or two standard, multipurpose pans for stir frying—the Chinese *wok*, which means "pot," or a heavy skillet. In either case, avoid Teflon, Silverstone, and other such nonstick linings, because they are useless at the high heats required for stir frying and will quickly lose their nonstick properties.

The Wok

The typical wok is a large spun steel pan, either round or flat-bottomed, with high sloping sides and two handles (see page 16). These handles normally are a pair of metal grips that you take hold of with a potholder or mitt, or the wok may have one short straight handle to grasp with a potholder and one long handle, sometimes covered with wood, that stays cool enough to hold with your bare hand.

A round-bottomed wok works best on the open flame of a gas range. Gas will heat the bottom and sides of the wok quickly and uniformly, and the flame can be adjusted easily to keep the wok from overheating.

However, if you have an electric range with either flat coils or a smooth Corningware-type surface, a round-bottomed pan is dangerous; it may tip over on the flat cooking surface. Also, it will not work effectively because electric heat is more difficult to control. Your best strategy is to use a flat-bottomed wok or a large, heavy skillet, both of which will conduct heat more efficiently from a flat heat source.

Note: even a flat-bottomed cooking pan will tend to overheat quickly on a very hot burner, or, at the other extreme, it will cool down too fast if you take it off the stove momentarily. You can compensate by watching the food with special care and by *anticipating* the need for temperature changes: don't wait until the oil is smoking before slightly lowering the heat. Try lifting the wok off the burner from time to time. Another tip: when you start cooking, use two burners. Set one of them at high heat and the other at medium high, and switch back and forth as you cook.

Chopsticks

You may prefer to eat your Chinese meals with a knife and fork. But chopsticks are perfectly designed for picking up small pieces of meat and vegetables from a plate or a soup bowl, as well as for bringing small bites of rice from bowl to mouth. They come in a variety of materials, from wood to ivory. The standard length is 12 inches. If you cannot find them locally, the mail-order houses listed on page 103 can supply them at reasonable cost. The diagram here illustrates the basic position for holding chopsticks with the fingers. The bottom stick braces, and the top one moves.

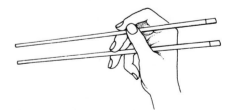

Chopsticks are the best possible tool not only for eating Chinese food but for stir frying or deep frying. For cooking use, buy 16-inch wooden chopsticks, two or three pairs at a minimum.

Woks come in a variety of materials, including copper, which is a good heat conductor but very expensive. The best material, as well as the most economical, is spun carbon steel, which conducts heat very well and is conveniently lightweight. Cast iron is a very good material because it is heat-tempered, but it is also heavy to handle. Avoid stainless steel, which will overheat and cause food to burn.

Many professional cooks say that a wok with one long and one short handle is the most convenient, but you should follow your own preference. Though woks range in diameter from 12 to 24 inches, the most versatile pan is 14 inches across and 4½ inches deep. The recipes in this volume are all easily prepared in a 14-inch wok.

Round-bottomed woks come with a separate, circular metal stand to support the wok securely above the flame. A wok must also have a lid, and most come with a domed lid for steaming and for keeping food warm after cooking.

Whether you shop for your wok in a department store or in a kitchen supply house, you will probably also find electric woks for sale. These are sometimes useful for steaming (see page 13) but unsatisfactory for stir frying. They have the same disadvantages as electric heat: you cannot maneuver the wok to correct the flow of heat from the source.

Preparing and Maintaining the Wok

Before stir frying in a new wok, you must clean and season it. The "seasoning" is a coat of oil permanently baked onto the interior to prevent food from sticking to the surface. Because most woks come from the manufacturer with a machine-oil coating, wash the wok inside and out with hot water and detergent, and dry it.

Then, pour a tablespoon of liquid cooking oil (corn, peanut, or any vegetable oil) into a small bowl and set out a pastry brush or a wadded paper towel. Place the wok over very high heat, making sure it heats all over, right up to the rim. Dip the pastry brush or paper towel into the oil and coat the interior of the wok slowly and thoroughly. Wipe off any excess. Remove it from the heat to cool for about 10 minutes. Then repeat the heating, oiling, and cooling process once or twice more until a black spot appears in the bottom of the wok. You are now ready to cook with it. Be sure to wipe out the wok with hot water and a sponge immediately after using it for the first time. Eventually, through repeated use, the whole interior of the wok should turn a lustrous black.

To clean a wok after cooking, use only hot water and a sponge or soft-bristled dishwashing brush. Avoid scouring with a stiff-bristled brush or using detergents; you will remove the seasoning coat. And never use powdered cleanser or abrasive pads; these will scratch the surface and cause food to stick. If the wok gets so greasy after a large amount of deep frying that you have to wash it with soap, use only a tiny amount and if necessary reseason it afterward, as directed. If you buy a cast iron wok, dry it carefully after each use to prevent rusting.

The Skillet

A heavy cast iron skillet is the best for stir frying because cast iron will evenly distribute and retain heat. Like the wok, the iron skillet needs to be seasoned. To clean the skillet after cooking, wipe it with coarse salt and a paper towel. If you must wash it, use the smallest possible amount of soap—don't use scouring pads—and dry it thoroughly.

Most recipes in this book call for a heavy-gauge 12-inch skillet. Buy one with either a domed glass or a cast iron cover.

Other Stir-Frying Tools

If you are expert at handling chopsticks, a pair of 16-inch long ones make a good stir-frying tool. A long-handled wood or metal wok spatula or spoon and a slotted spoon will also do, and either will double as a scoop if you want to remove food without upending the pan.

The Oil

The recipes in this book call for corn or peanut oil, usually less than 4 tablespoons, in a stir fry. Other fats such as butter and olive oil are unacceptable because they burn at high temperatures, and, like solid shortening, they are not traditionally Chinese flavors. But corn, peanut, and safflower oils have just the right clean aroma and taste. Most recipes tell you to heat the wok or skillet before adding the oil. This helps to create a smooth, nonstick cooking surface.

Rice

Rice is the customary accompaniment to most Chinese meals and the simplest of all side dishes to cook. Once you have mastered the technique, you will not need a recipe.

The Chinese eat many types of rice—long-grained, short-grained, round, and flat—but long-grain white rice cooks up drier and fluffier, with each cooked grain remaining separate, and is also less starchy than other kinds. The directions on whatever brand you buy will no doubt advise against rinsing the rice before cooking. A Chinese chef, nevertheless, always rinses rice thoroughly in cold water, not once but five or six times, on the theory that rice tastes fresher and less starchy when rinsed. If you buy a standard American long-grain rice, uncoated with any kind of additive, you may skip the rinsing without sacrificing either quality or cleanliness.

One cup of uncooked rice yields slightly less than four cups of cooked—the amount specified for the menus in this volume. When a menu calls for rice, you will be referred to the following recipe.

Perfect Rice

2 cups cold water
1 cup raw long-grain rice

1. Add the water and rice to a medium-size saucepan. Heat uncovered until water comes to a full boil.
2. Turn heat to low and cover. Simmer rice for 20 minutes without stirring.
3. Remove pot from heat and let it stand 5 to 10 minutes.
4. Remove cover and fluff rice with a fork before serving.

You will note that some of the cooks in this volume have slightly different ways of gauging the temperature or readiness of the wok (or skillet) and the oil. Some, like Ken Hom, suggest that a wok is ready when it takes on a rainbowlike appearance, whereas Barbara Tropp's method is to see whether a bead of water evaporates on contact with the wok. Others simply tell you to heat the wok for 1 minute.

These methods are all acceptable, and here is one other: First heat the wok or skillet over high heat for about 1 minute. When a drop of water sizzles immediately on contact, add the oil. Then wait 30 to 90 seconds, depending on your stove, and put a sliver of food in the pan. If it foams at once, you are ready to stir fry.

Cooking with Oil: Deep Frying

This technique is known in almost every nation and in some ways is similar to stir frying. You immerse small batches of food cut into small pieces in very hot oil until crisp on the outside and cooked through within.

Because the temperature of the oil for deep frying is critical, a deep-fat thermometer is a must. As you gain experience in deep frying, however, you will be able to gauge the temperature by the appearance of the oil or by testing a bit of food. At 275 degrees, the oil has small swirls and subsurface eddies but is not bubbling, and a small piece of food dropped into the pan will sink to the bottom and begin cooking at once. At 375 degrees, the oil gives off a slight haze, and food added at this time will rise to the top, surrounded by bubbles. At 400 degrees—the temperature for a very quick fry—the oil is just below the smoking point and gives off a thicker haze. A piece of food will rise quickly to the surface, covered by white foam, and will brown immediately. Do not linger, or the oil may burn. Begin cooking at once.

Utensils for Deep Frying

A properly seasoned wok is as good for deep-frying as for stir frying, but it can be dangerous because of the likelihood of spills. A Dutch oven or any good-quality pan with high sides and a heavy bottom is much safer. A stainless steel Dutch oven with a copper or aluminum bottom is efficient and easy to clean. Cast iron deep fryers are very effective but difficult to handle because of their weight. If you do not own one, you may wish to buy an electric deep fryer with a thermostatic control, although none of the recipes in this volume requires it.

You will also need a tool for removing the cooked food from the hot oil: long chopsticks or long-handled tongs. You may also use a long-handled, slotted metal spoon or a Chinese long-handled mesh spoon (see page 17).

Also necessary for deep frying are paper towels, folded and stacked in 3 or 4 layers, for draining food as it comes from the hot oil. No matter how quick the deep-frying process is, you must immediately drain foods cooked in this way, or they will absorb excess oil as they cool and become soggy and unappetizing. Nothing soaks up oil quite as conveniently as paper towels, but paper napkins or a stack of 2 or 3 thin, inexpensive paper plates will also do the job.

Deep Frying Oil

Use the same oil for deep frying that you would for stir frying: a liquid vegetable oil, preferably corn or peanut. Be sure to use as much oil as your recipe calls for.

You can economize, however, by reusing the same oil for a number of different meals, provided you have not scorched it. After deep frying, let the oil cool completely, and then pour it through a fine-mesh strainer lined with double-folded cheesecloth into a storage container. Store in a cool pantry if you deep fry often, or in your refrigerator. Add fresh oil at each reuse. You can keep reusing it 5 or 6 times, as long as it continues to smell and taste fresh. Once it turns dark brown, discard it.

Cooking with Oil: Oil Blanching or Velvetizing

This technique, essential to many Chinese dishes, is unlike any Occidental cooking method. It is a form of precooking, usually in oil heated to 275 degrees. The purpose is to prepare the food for quick-cooking at a later stage.

When the oil is hot enough, add the food—usually strips or shreds of meat or vegetables—and stir to separate the pieces. Red meats should cook just long enough to lose their redness; chicken should turn opaque; vegetables take on a vibrant, velvety color. Remove the foods and drain on paper towels.

Cooking with Water: Steaming

Next to stir frying, steaming is the most common technique in Chinese cooking. Quick and economical, like stir frying, steaming beautifully retains the color, vitamins, and natural flavors of foods. It is also easy because foods set to steam need less attention. Make sure the water is boiling before you set the food in the pot, because the high heat acts to seal in the flavor of the food. Check occasionally to make sure the water has not boiled off.

Utensils for Steaming

All you need is a large pot with a lid, a heatproof platter or dish to set inside the pot, and a trivet for holding the food above the level of the boiling water. The Chinese often use two- or three-tiered bamboo steamers, setting them above boiling water in a wok. The bamboo steamer is so attractive that you can bring one tier of it to the table when it is time to serve the meal. You may also like the convenience and durability of a two- or three-tiered, Western-style aluminum or stainless steel steamer pot. It works in exactly the same way as the wok–bamboo steamer combination: the steam from the boiling water in the bottom tier rises into the two upper tiers through perforations. The lid traps the steam within, where it has enough room to circulate.

You can improvise a simple tiered steamer very readily, as shown below. Almost any large covered cooking pot will do. Find a perforated rack, a colander, or a wire basket that will fit inside the pan and at the same time hold the food above water level without letting any of it fall through. The pot cover should still fit tightly over the steaming pot.

IMPROVISED STEAMER

Cooking with Water: Blanching

Like deep frying, this technique is common to most of the world's cuisines. Blanching is passing vegetables through boiling water to prepare them for later cooking, which in this volume usually means stir frying. A recipe that calls for blanching will give you the amount of water and the precooking time—usually only a few seconds. Generally, blanching shortens the stir-fry process and "sets" the color of the vegetables, making them more attractive when cooked and giving them an interesting, rich texture. When you remove the blanched vegetables from the hot water, rinse them in a colander with very cold water to stop the cooking, or plunge them into a bowl of ice water. Drain them and pat them dry with towels. Blanched vegetables should be completely dry before you add them to a stir fry; otherwise they will cause the oil to spatter.

Making Stock

Canned stock, either chicken or beef, is acceptable for most Chinese sauces but may add salt that you do not want. Homemade stocks have a rich flavor that is hard to match and the additional advantage of your being able to control the saltiness. Meat trimmings, bones, and raw vegetable pieces can also go into the stockpot. As you slice and chop for a stir fry, gather any rejected but still usable pieces of meat and vegetable and put them in a plastic bag. You can freeze them, accumulating more as time passes, and then have a rainy-day stock-making session. Stock freezes well and will keep for three months in the freezer. Use small containers for convenience and freeze in premeasured amounts: a cup or half a cup. Or pour the cooled stock into ice cube trays, then remove the frozen cubes and store in a plastic bag. You can drop these frozen cubes directly into your saucepan.

An authentic Chinese stock uses a whole chicken for flavoring. The stock cooks for 4 hours, but if you wish to save time, you may disjoint the chicken and obtain a perfectly good stock in just 2 hours. Be sure to include the neck, gizzard, and liver for a richer flavor.

Chinese Chicken Stock

1 whole roasting chicken (about 2½ pounds)
1 whole scallion

1 small chunk fresh ginger, sliced into quarter-sized rounds
2 slices Chinese dried orange peel (optional)
Salt

1. Clean chicken, removing excess fat. Rinse well to rid it of any clinging connective tissue or blood clots.
2. Place chicken in stockpot filled with 2 quarts water or water to cover.
3. Trim off scallion root and add scallion, ginger, and orange peel, if using, to pot.
4. Bring to a boil, then lower heat and cover. Simmer 4 hours, stirring occasionally.
5. If you have time, allow to cool before straining. Place a colander or strainer lined with a triple thickness of cheesecloth or strong paper towels over a large pot. Pour in the stock and discard the bones and chicken.
6. Season to taste but sparingly; the stock may be the base of a sauced stir-fry dish that does not need salt.
7. To remove accumulated fat, use a broad spoon tilted at an angle or paper towels to carefully skim the surface until the broth is clear.
8. When the stock has cooled, you may freeze it. Or it will keep under refrigeration up to 3 days. Before using, reheat it and allow to boil for 2 minutes.

Pantry (for this volume)

A well-stocked, properly organized pantry is a time-saver for anyone who wants to prepare great meals in the shortest possible time. Location is the critical factor for staple storage. Whether your pantry consists of a small refrigerator and two or three shelves over the sink or a large freezer, refrigerator, and whole room just off the kitchen, you must protect staples from heat and light. In maintaining or restocking your pantry, follow these rules:

1. Store staples by kind and date. Canned goods need a separate shelf or a separate spot on the shelf. Put the oldest cans in front, so that you need not examine each one as you pull it out. Keep track of refrigerated and frozen staples by jotting the date on the package or writing it on a bit of masking tape.

2. Store flour, sugar, and other dry ingredients in canisters or in jars with tight lids, where they will last for months. Glass or clear plastic allows you to see at a glance how much remains.

3. Keep a running grocery list near where you cook, so that when a staple such as cooking oil, sugar, or flour is half gone, you will be sure to stock up.

ON THE SHELF:

Baking powder

Baking soda

Bamboo shoots

Bean curd, fermented and bottled

Black beans, canned or packaged

Chinese fermented black beans, also known as Chinese salted black beans, come canned or in plastic bags. After opening them, store in the refrigerator.

Chicken (or beef) stock, homemade or canned

Chili paste, bottled

Chinese baby corn, canned

Before using, rinse in cool water and drain. Store in the refrigerator.

Cornstarch

An effective binder in marinades for poultry, meat, and fish as well as a common Chinese thickening agent, instead of flour, in sauces.

Duck sauce

Also called plum sauce, this condiment is made from plums, apricots, vinegar, chili, and sugar.

Flour

All-purpose, bleached or unbleached.

Herbs and spices

cinnamon, ground

five-spice powder (or five-fragrance powder)

This mixture includes cloves, cinnamon, Szechwan peppercorns, fennel, and star anise. You can make your own by blending roughly equal portions of these spices. Store as you would any spice.

mustard, dry

orange peel, dried

Buy only the Chinese variety, sold in jars.

pepper

Cayenne pepper, ground
crushed red pepper
dried red chili peppers
dried red pepper flakes
hot red peppers, fresh or dried
Szechwan peppercorns

These aromatic, mild brown peppercorns are available in specialty shops and Chinese groceries. When cooking, use them whole, and store in an airtight container.

white pepper, ground

Tastes like black pepper but has been ground without the black skin. Use in dishes when black specks would spoil the appearance.

salt

table salt
Kosher salt

This coarse salt, with no additives, has a superior flavor and texture.

sesame seeds, raw

A crunchy and delicious garnish for many Chinese dishes. Toast in the oven (or in a dry skillet over moderate heat) to bring out their nutty flavor.

star anise

Star anise, like Western anise, is licorice flavored but is stronger. The pod is brown and star-shaped, with eight points. Use it whole as a garnish, or break it up for greater flavor, as the recipe directs.

***Hoisin* sauce**

A sweet soybean-based sauce with vinegar and spices, it keeps indefinitely if refrigerated.

Honey

Hot pepper sauce

Mushrooms

black mushrooms, dried

A staple of the Chinese kitchen, these will keep almost forever, and most markets carry them. To restore their flavor and shape, cover them with boiling water and soak for 20 to 30 minutes. Be sure to buy the Chinese variety, which differ in flavor and appearance from the Western.

straw mushrooms, canned

These slippery, brown mushrooms—milder than dried ones—are about an inch long and have a pleasant texture and flavor.

tree ear mushrooms, dried

Also called cloud ears or tree fungus, these crinkly, delicately flavored mushrooms are smaller than dried black ones but puff up when soaked in water.

Nuts

almonds

peanuts, dry-roasted, unsalted

pine nuts

Oils

Oriental sesame oil

Sold in bottles and cans, this highly aromatic oil is for garnishing, not cooking. Always buy Japanese or Chinese brands, which differ from the Middle Eastern varieties. Store in a cool cupboard; if you refrigerate it, do return it to room temperature before using.

sesame chili oil

This spicy flavoring agent is corn, peanut, or sesame oil seasoned with hot red peppers. This will keep indefinitely when stored in a dark, cool place.

vegetable oils

Any good brand of corn, peanut, or safflower oil will do for Chinese frying, or you may mix them. Avoid cottonseed and soybean oils, which may give food an oily, unpleasant flavor. Vegetable oils will keep almost indefinitely on the shelf.

Onions

Store all dry-skinned onions in a cool, dry place.

Bermuda onion

Whether white or yellow, these are always large. Milder and sweeter than the ordinary yellow or white cooking onion.

scallions

Also called green onions. Mild in flavor. Use the white bulbs as well as the green tops. Store in the refrigerator or chop coarsely, wrap in plastic, and freeze.

shallots

A sweet and delicate cross between onions and garlic. Best when chopped. Buy the largest you can find because they are easier to peel and chop.

Oriental barbecue sauce, in jars

Oyster sauce, in jars or cans

A rich brown sauce that is made from ground oysters and other ingredients and frequently used in Cantonese recipes. Available in bottles, it keeps indefinitely in the refrigerator.

Pastas, dried

Chinese rice noodles

Italian spaghettini or vermicelli

Peanut butter

Plum sauce (see Duck sauce)

Rice, long-grain white

Sesame paste, in jars

A dark brown aromatic paste made of toasted sesame seeds. Excellent for flavoring cold noodle dishes.

Shrimp, dried

Available in specialty shops in packages or jars. Their smell is sharp and fishy, but they are delicious when prepared. There is no substitute.

Soy Sauce

Extracted from fermented soybeans, light and dark soy sauces come in a range of flavors and brands. The so-called light soy sauce is actually very brown. Japanese-style (not necessarily imported from Japan) soys are the best because they are less salty than the Chinese. Dark soy sauces, though actually no browner than the "light," are sweeter, saltier, and more concentrated in flavor— very good occasionally but less generally useful than the light variety.

Sugar, white and brown

Tahini, canned

Middle Eastern paste made from ground, hulled sesame seeds.

Tientsin preserved vegetable, canned

Also called Szechwan pickle, this is celery cabbage preserved with garlic, spices, and salt.

Tomatoes

Italian plum tomatoes, canned

Catsup

Vinegars

The Chinese make vinegars from a fermented base of rice and fruits, and age them in a variety of ways for different colors and flavors. This volume also calls for some standard Western vinegars.

Chinese black vinegar (Italian balsamic vinegar is an acceptable substitute.)

Chinese dark vinegar

Chinese red vinegar

rice vinegar, Chinese or Japanese

Chinese red rice vinegar unseasoned Chinese or Japanese rice vinegar

rice wine vinegar, Chinese or Japanese

white distilled vinegar

wine vinegars, red and white

Water chestnut powder

The starch of dried, powdered chestnuts, it is useful for lightly coating foods before deep frying and gives a more luminous cast to foods than does cornstarch, which is an acceptable substitute.

Water chestnuts, canned

Fresh in flavor and crunchy in texture, they are the bulbs of an Asian marsh plant, not chestnuts at all.

Wines/Spirits

Chinese rice wine

dry sherry

dry white wine

ginger wine

Worcestershire sauce

IN THE REFRIGERATOR:

Bean curd

Tofu or bean curd is a custardlike cake of pureed soybeans, bland tasting but an excellent protein source. Sold in squares in Oriental markets and at many supermarket produce counters, it must be stored in water. It will stay fresh in the refrigerator if you change the water daily.

Bean sprouts

The best kind are the familiar mung bean sprouts, a staple in Chinese and Japanese restaurants and now available at most supermarket produce counters. Refrigerated in a plastic bag, they will stay fresh for several days.

Cabbage

Bok choy, with crisp white stalks and dark green leaves, and Napa, which has wrinkled, pale green leaves, are the two kinds of Chinese cabbage.

Coriander

Also called Chinese *cilantro* or, in Spanish markets, *culantro*, this pungent herb tastes nothing like American parsley. Taste it raw to see whether its unusual flavor appeals to you. If not, cut down the amount you use in any recipe that calls for it.

Fresh ginger

Slice only what you need and peel each slice. The remainder will stay fresh for at least a week in a plastic bag in the refrigerator. It will keep indefinitely when stored and refrigerated in a jar with sherry to cover. Powdered ginger is not a substitute.

Smithfield ham

Real Chinese ham is almost impossible to find, but Smithfield comes closest to it in flavor. Italian prosciutto is another substitute. Tightly wrapped in foil and refrigerated, either ham will keep for weeks.

Equipment

Proper cooking equipment makes the work light and is a good cook's most prized possession. You can cook expertly without a store-bought steamer or even a food processor, but basic pans, knives, and a few other items are indispensable. Below are the things you need and some attractive options for preparing the menus in this volume.

Pots and pans
5-quart Dutch oven with cover
Large pot (for cooking noodles)
Wok, 14-inch, with cover
Heavy saucepans, 1 with tight-fitting cover for cooking rice (1-,2-, and 3-quart capacities)
Heavy-gauge 12-inch skillet with cover
Heavy-gauge 7-inch skillet
Steamer
  Bamboo, aluminum, collapsible vegetable, or homemade are all acceptable.
9-inch pie plate to fit inside steamer (glass or heatproof)
Broiling pan
Roasting pan with rack or metal trivet
9-by-12-inch baking sheet

Knives and cleavers
  Except for chopping through bone, a chef's knife will do almost anything a cleaver can, but a set of cleavers (heavy, medium, and light) is traditional Chinese equipment. Care for them as you would fine knives: hone them frequently, avoid putting them in the dishwasher or leaving them loose in drawers, wash and dry them after each use, and store them in a case or holder that will protect the edge.
Chef's knife, 10-inch blade
Cleavers, heavy, medium, and light
Paring knife
Sharpening steel
Knife rack
  (wall-mounted magnetic type or wooden for the countertop)
  It is not advisable to store your cleavers this way.

Other cooking tools
Chopping board
Mixing bowls in graduated sizes (large, medium, and small)
Skewers (preferably bamboo)

Soup tureen or individual bowls
Soup bowls
Sauceboat
Spatulas
Metal wok spatula
Slotted spatula
Slotted metal spoon, or Chinese mesh spoon
2 long-handled wooden spoons
Soup ladle
Long-tined fork
16-inch chopsticks
Strainer
Metal colander
2 sets of measuring cups and spoons in graduated sizes
Cutting board/chopping block (wood or acrylic)
Meat pounder or mallet
Deep-fat thermometer
Kitchen parchment
  You may substitute aluminum foil.
Paper towels
Scissors, small embroidery type
Tea strainer
Small wire whisk
Vegetable peeler

Electrical Appliances
Food processor or blender

Optional
Hand mixer
Salad spinner
Melon baller
Zester

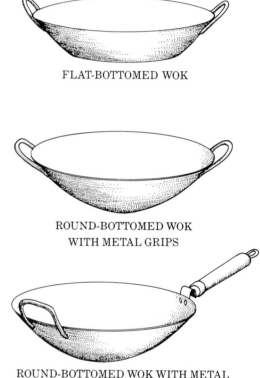

FLAT-BOTTOMED WOK

ROUND-BOTTOMED WOK
WITH METAL GRIPS

ROUND-BOTTOMED WOK WITH METAL
GRIP AND WOOD-COVERED HANDLE

METAL WOK SPATULA

9-BY-12-INCH BAKING SHEET

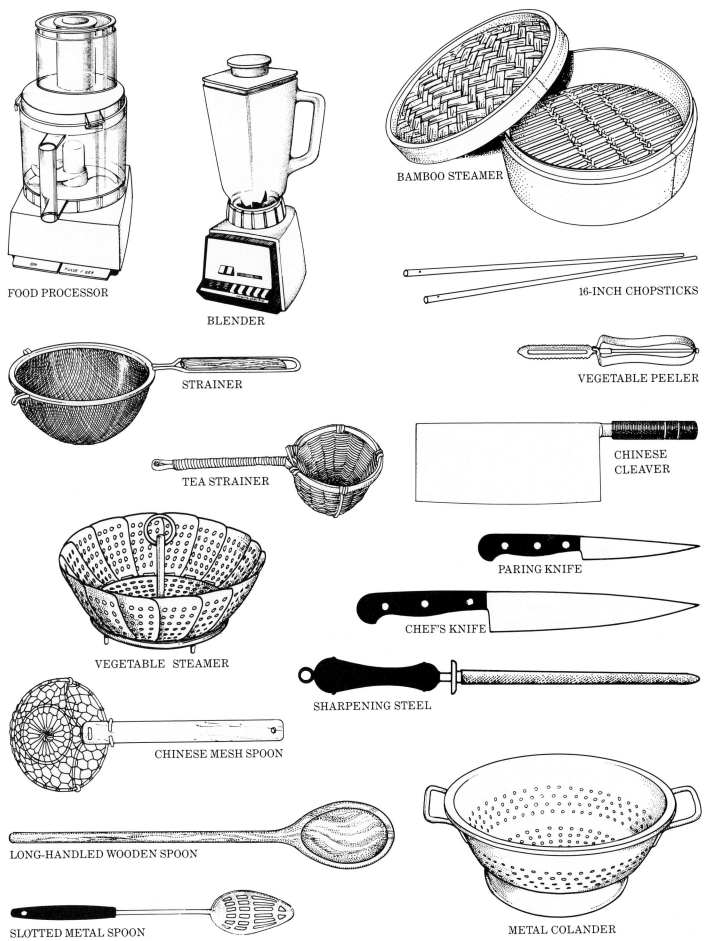

FOOD PROCESSOR

BLENDER

BAMBOO STEAMER

16-INCH CHOPSTICKS

STRAINER

VEGETABLE PEELER

TEA STRAINER

CHINESE CLEAVER

VEGETABLE STEAMER

PARING KNIFE

CHEF'S KNIFE

SHARPENING STEEL

CHINESE MESH SPOON

LONG-HANDLED WOODEN SPOON

SLOTTED METAL SPOON

METAL COLANDER

17

Jean Yueh

A native of Shanghai, Jean Yueh learned to cook professionally in Hong Kong, and her three menus reflect this southern-eastern approach. She blends the cooking techniques of these two regions and applies them to ingredients easily available in American supermarkets. Like all good Chinese cooks, Jean Yueh emphasizes the freshest possible ingredients, so the techniques she uses here retain natural colors and nutrients.

Menu 1, with meat-stuffed zucchini, and Menu 3, with poached fish and chicken and spinach soup, are typical dishes of the eastern region. Menu 2 features a Cantonese favorite—lemon chicken. Each meal has contrasting textures but harmonizing flavors.

Jean Yueh's meals are fun to prepare, and they will help you to develop your skills, since she demonstrates a spectrum of techniques: poaching, steaming, blanching, stir frying, and deep frying. In her classes and her cookbooks, she simplifies her classic Chinese recipes by using modern kitchen appliances, such as the food processor, though she never sacrifices taste and appearance for the sake of speed.

In addition to its use as a cooking tool, a Chinese bamboo steamer is also a handsome serving dish for this stuffed zucchini. Or you can use any attractive plate or platter, lined with lettuce leaves. If the meal is informal, bring the stir-fried bean curd to the table in the wok or sauté pan and serve the rice in small bowls.

Stuffed Zucchini
Home-Style Bean Curd
Rice

Stuffed zucchini is a home-style Shanghai summer dish. Although Shanghai and the whole eastern region are known for their long-simmered dishes, the region abounds, too, in fish and fresh produce, which chefs cook quickly. This zucchini stuffed with ground pork is light and delicious—first steamed, then glazed with a brown sauce. It is especially good served with a bean curd dish.

Bean curd, also called "tofu," is an economical and adaptable food that is a Chinese staple. Made from soy beans, tofu has many merits: it is full of protein and vitamins, and low in cholesterol. Served alone, tofu tastes bland, but it readily absorbs flavors from accompanying sauces or other ingredients. Firm tofu, which this recipe calls for, holds its shape so that it can be cut up or stir fried without disintegrating. Avoid using soft bean curd, which will not work in this particular recipe. This home-style bean curd dish acquires a golden brown crust while remaining tender and moist within. Hot spices are not typical of the eastern region, but if you like spicy food, use the hot dried pepper or crushed red pepper flakes that Jean Yueh lists as optional.

WHAT TO DRINK

These dishes present a range of delicate, fresh flavors best complemented by a simple, light wine. An Italian Pinot Grigio, a California Pinot Blanc, or a German wine from the Moselle are all good choices.

SHOPPING LIST AND STAPLES

1 pound lean ground pork or boneless pork loin or butt
1 pound fresh firm bean curd
2 zucchini (about 2 inches in diameter and 1¼ pounds total weight)
1 medium-size green bell pepper
1 medium-size red bell pepper
2 hot dried red peppers, or ½ teaspoon dried red pepper flakes (optional)
1 bunch scallions
Coriander or Italian parsley sprigs (optional)
1 small head romaine lettuce (optional)
Fresh ginger
8-ounce can water chestnuts
¾ cup Chinese Chicken Stock (see page 13)
4 tablespoons corn, peanut, or vegetable oil
1 tablespoon Oriental sesame oil (optional)

1 tablespoon dark soy sauce
3½ tablespoons plus 2 teaspoons light soy sauce, plus another 2 teaspoons (optional)
1 cup uncooked rice
2 tablespoons plus ½ teaspoon cornstarch, plus another ½ teaspoon (optional)
1 teaspoon sugar
1 tablespoon dry sherry

UTENSILS

Food processor
Wok
    or 10-inch skillet (for bean curd)
    and small saucepan (for zucchini glaze, optional)
12-inch skillet
    or bamboo steamer (for zucchini)
Medium-size saucepan with cover (for rice)
Large bowl
Medium-size bowl
10-inch glass pie plate or other heatproof plate
Metal colander
1-inch metal trivet (for steaming, if using skillet)
Measuring cups and spoons
Chinese cleaver or chef's knife
Paring knife
Slotted metal spoon
Melon ball cutter (optional)

START-TO-FINISH STEPS

1. Follow general rice recipe on page 12, steps 1 and 2.
2. Chop scallion, mince ginger, and drain water chestnuts. Follow zucchini recipe step 1.
3. Follow bean curd recipe steps 1 and 2. Preheat oven to 200 degrees.
4. Follow zucchini recipe steps 2 through 8. While zucchini are steaming, slice fresh ginger and drained water chestnuts for bean curd recipe. Follow recipe steps 3 and 4.
5. When zucchini are cooked, keep warm in oven. Follow general rice recipe step 3.
6. If glazing zucchini, follow zucchini recipe step 9 and keep warm while cooking bean curd.
7. Wipe out wok. Follow bean curd recipe steps 5 through 7. Follow general rice recipe step 4.
8. Remove zucchini from oven. Complete zucchini recipe step 10 and serve with bean curd and rice.

RECIPES

Stuffed Zucchini

1 pound lean ground pork, or boneless pork loin or butt
    ground in food processor
1 scallion, finely chopped
1 teaspoon finely minced fresh ginger
5 large water chestnuts, drained and minced
1 tablespoon plus ½ teaspoon cornstarch
1 tablespoon dry sherry
1½ tablespoons plus 2 teaspoons light soy sauce
1 teaspoon sugar
2 zucchini (about 2 inches in diameter and 1¼ pounds
    total weight)
Fresh coriander or Italian parsley sprigs for garnish
    (optional)
Romaine lettuce leaves for garnish (optional)

For glaze (optional):
2 teaspoons light soy sauce
½ teaspoon cornstarch mixed with 1 teaspoon water
Chinese Chicken Stock, if necessary

1. In large bowl, combine ground pork, scallion, ginger, water chestnuts, 1 tablespoon cornstarch, dry sherry, 1½ tablespoons soy sauce, and sugar. Mix thoroughly.
2. Wash zucchini. Cut off both ends, then cut each zucchini crosswise into 8 rounds about 1 inch thick.
3. Use paring knife, teaspoon, or melon ball cutter to scoop out small hollow from each zucchini section. Do not cut all the way through and leave rim about ¼ inch thick.
4. Bring 1 inch water to a boil in heavy 12-inch skillet or, if using bamboo steamer, in wok.
5. Spoon portion of pork mixture into each zucchini section, mounding slightly. With moistened fingers, smooth top of filling.
6. Arrange stuffed zucchini in 10-inch glass pie plate or other heatproof rimmed dish at least 1 inch smaller in diameter than skillet or in bamboo steamer, if using.
7. Set plate of stuffed zucchini on trivet over boiling water in skillet. Or you may place stuffed zucchini in bamboo steamer set in wok with water just below level of steamer. (For bamboo steaming method, see page 13).
8. Steam over medium-high heat about 20 minutes, or until meat is cooked and zucchini are still slightly crisp. Test by tasting. Cook longer if you prefer very soft zucchini. You may serve zucchini at this point, or transfer cooked zucchini to serving platter and keep warm in oven while you prepare glaze that follows.
9. Measure ¼ cup liquid from plate on which zucchini were steamed. If necessary, add enough chicken stock to make ¼ cup. Place liquid in wok or small saucepan. Add 2 teaspoons soy sauce. Slowly stir cornstarch mixture into sauce. Heat to boiling, or until thin, translucent glaze is formed.
10. Pour sauce evenly over zucchini. Garnish with sprigs of coriander or Italian parsley, if desired. For serving in bamboo steamer, line tray with fresh lettuce leaves and arrange zucchini on top.

Home-Style Bean Curd

1 pound fresh firm bean curd
1 medium-size green bell pepper
1 medium-size red bell pepper
5 water chestnuts, drained and sliced in ¼-inch rounds
2 scallions, cut in 1-inch sections
2 slices fresh ginger, about ⅛ inch thick
¾ cup Chinese Chicken Stock
2 tablespoons light soy sauce, or to taste
1 tablespoon dark soy sauce
1 tablespoon cornstarch
4 tablespoons corn, peanut, or vegetable oil
2 hot dried red peppers, or ½ teaspoon dried red pepper
    flakes (optional)
1 tablespoon Oriental sesame oil (optional)

1. Drain bean curd in colander. If using 3-inch squares of bean curd, cut each piece into 4 equal triangles. If using vacuum-sealed 1-pound block, cut into 4 equal pieces, then cut each piece into 2 equal triangles. Slice each triangle into half its thickness. There will be 16 triangles.
2. Blot bean curd triangles. Place on double layers of paper towels and press to absorb excess moisture.
3. Wash peppers and core. Remove seeds, halve, and cut peppers into 1-inch strips, then into 1-inch squares.
4. For sauce, stir to combine chicken stock, light and dark soy sauce, and cornstarch in medium-size bowl.
5. Heat wok or 10-inch skillet, then add cooking oil and heat on high until very hot. Fry bean curd and cook until both sides are golden brown, about 5 minutes. Remove bean curd with slotted spoon and keep warm in preheated 200-degree oven.
6. Reheat wok or skillet, adding more oil if less than 2 tablespoons remain. Add hot dried red peppers, if you are using them, or dried red pepper flakes, ginger, and scallions, and cook 30 seconds over medium heat. Discard hot peppers (not necessary if using red pepper flakes) and ginger. Add green and red bell peppers and water chestnuts. Stir fry 1 to 2 minutes, then add bean curd.
7. Stir soy sauce mixture thoroughly and add to pan. Stir constantly over high heat until sauce is thickened. Add sesame oil if desired and stir to mix. Serve hot.

ADDED TOUCH

For an easy appetizer, toast shelled whole pecan pieces in a 350-degree oven 10 minutes, then cool to room temperature. Spread ¼ teaspoon *hoisin* sauce or to taste over a small leaf of iceberg lettuce. Let each person wrap 2 to 3 pecan pieces in the lettuce leaf. For dessert, top lemon sherbet with coffee liqueur and sprinkle with grated lemon rind.

Lemon Chicken
Stir-Fried Carrots and Zucchini
Rice

Breaded chicken breasts in lemon sauce with a stir fry of fresh vegetables make a delicate combination that you can serve on a single large platter. Light colors and clear glassware provide the right setting for this meal.

Hong Kong, the culinary center of the Orient, excels in the dishes of southern China, and one of the best of these is lemon chicken. The version here, with a cornstarch batter and a sauce flavored with fresh lemon juice and soy, is light and easy to make. Some Hong Kong chefs use butter to enrich the sauce for this dish, though this is far from customary Chinese cooking. If you like a buttery sauce, follow their example and swirl in a tablespoon of unsalted butter as you finish making the sauce.

For additional flavor and color, garnish the chicken with a combination of finely shredded lemon rind and carrot. Before juicing the lemons for the sauce, peel them lightly, without cutting into the white pith, and shred the strips.

To prepare the vegetables for stir frying, you need a very sharp knife, preferably a Chinese cleaver, to cut them precisely into neat matchstick-size pieces. The dish looks more attractive if the shreds are uniform, and the vegetables will cook through evenly. Because carrots are firm and require a slightly longer cooking time, you must stir fry them before adding the zucchini to the wok.

WHAT TO DRINK

A chilled dry white wine goes well with lemon chicken. Try a Chardonnay (imported or domestic), which adapts to tart flavors. Beer or tea are also good choices.

SHOPPING LIST AND STAPLES

3 whole skinless, boneless chicken breasts (about 1½ pounds)
1 pound zucchini
¾ pound carrots
1 head iceberg lettuce (optional)
1 large lemon for juice plus 2 lemons, sliced, for garnish (optional)
1 scallion
3 large eggs
1 tablespoon butter (optional)
4 cups plus 4 tablespoons corn, peanut, or vegetable oil
1 tablespoon plus 2 teaspoons light soy sauce
1 cup plus 2 tablespoons plus 1 teaspoon cornstarch
1 cup uncooked rice
5 tablespoons plus 1¼ teaspoons sugar
Salt
Freshly ground black pepper
2 teaspoons dry sherry

UTENSILS

Wok
  or 12-inch skillet
3-quart saucepan (for vegetable stir fry)
Medium-size saucepan with cover (for rice)
Small saucepan
9 by 12-inch baking sheet
3 medium-size bowls
Small bowl
Measuring cups and spoons
Chinese cleaver or chef's knife
Paring knife
Chinese mesh spoon or long-handled slotted metal spoon
Metal wok spatula or 2 wooden spoons
Wire whisk
Vegetable peeler
Deep-fat thermometer

START-TO-FINISH STEPS

In the morning: Follow lemon chicken recipe steps 1 through 4.
1. Bring chicken to room temperature 30 minutes before cooking.
2. Follow general rice recipe on page 12, steps 1 and 2.
3. Preheat oven to 200 degrees.
4. Follow carrots and zucchini recipe, steps 1 through 4. If you wish to serve hot, turn into heatproof serving dish and place in oven. Otherwise, let sit at room temperature.
5. Follow general rice recipe step 3.
6. Wipe out wok. Follow lemon chicken recipe steps 5 through 11.
7. Follow general rice recipe step 4. Remove carrots and zucchini from oven and serve with lemon chicken and rice.

RECIPES

Lemon Chicken

3 whole skinless, boneless chicken breasts
1½ teaspoons salt
¾ teaspoon sugar
¼ teaspoon freshly ground black pepper
2 teaspoons dry sherry
2 teaspoons light soy sauce
3 egg whites
1 cup plus 1 tablespoon cornstarch
4 cups corn, peanut, or vegetable oil
4 large leaves iceberg lettuce, washed and dried

Lemon sauce:
⅓ cup freshly squeezed lemon juice
1 tablespoon light soy sauce
¼ teaspoon salt, or to taste
5 tablespoons sugar, or to taste
4 teaspoons cornstarch
1 cup water

1 scallion, white part only, finely minced
1 tablespoon corn, peanut, or vegetable oil

1 tablespoon butter (optional)
2 lemons, sliced, for garnish (optional)

1. Cut each breast into halves. Detach small fillet underneath each half: you should have 2 large and 2 small pieces from each breast. Cut large pieces crosswise into halves.
2. In medium-size bowl, mix chicken thoroughly with salt, pepper, sugar, sherry, and soy sauce.
3. Beat egg whites until frothy. Put the cup of cornstarch in another medium-size bowl. Dip chicken, one piece at a time, into cornstarch, then into egg whites, then back into cornstarch until each piece is well coated.
4. Sprinkle the tablespoon of cornstarch on baking sheet. Place coated chicken in one layer on pan and refrigerate. (This can be done far in advance if time allows.)
5. Wash bowl in which chicken was marinated to use for sauce.
6. Heat 4 cups cooking oil to 375 degrees on deep-fat thermometer in wok or 3-quart saucepan.
7. If desired, finely shred lettuce leaves and spread evenly on serving platter.
8. Combine sauce ingredients in medium-size bowl.
9. When oil is hot, fry chicken a few pieces at a time, until coating is set and chicken is cooked, 3 to 5 minutes. Remove with Chinese mesh or slotted metal spoon to drain on plate lined with paper towels. For crisper chicken, fry it twice, but do not fully cook the first time. Keep chicken warm in preheated 200-degree oven.
10. Heat the 1 tablespoon of oil in small saucepan. Add finely minced scallion and cook 30 seconds. Stir lemon sauce mixture thoroughly to recombine the cornstarch and add to saucepan. Stir constantly until sauce is thickened and flows easily off spoon. Add butter, if desired, and stir to combine.
11. Cut chicken into ¾-inch strips and arrange neatly on top of the shredded lettuce. Drizzle half of lemon sauce over chicken. Pour remaining sauce into small bowl and serve with chicken. If desired, garnish with thinly sliced lemon and shredded lemon rind.

Stir-Fried Carrots and Zucchini

1 pound zucchini
¾ pound carrots
3 tablespoons corn, peanut, or vegetable oil
¾ teaspoon salt, or to taste
½ teaspoon sugar

1. Wash zucchini and trim off both ends. Cut zucchini diagonally into ¼-inch thick and 2-inch long oval slices. Stack a few slices and cut into ¼-inch shreds.
2. Peel carrots and cut similarly into ¼-inch shreds.
3. Heat wok or skillet until a bead of water immediately evaporates. Add oil and heat about 30 seconds, or until a carrot shred sizzles. Add carrots and stir fry to coat with oil. Cover and cook 2 to 3 minutes, stirring 2 or 3 times.
4. Add zucchini, salt, and sugar. Stir fry uncovered another minute, or until heated through. Serve hot or at room temperature.

Emerald Soup
Poached Fish Fillets, West Lake Style
Fresh Snow Pea Salad / Rice

Fish fillets, snow pea salad, rice, and soup provide a meal that is simple enough for children to enjoy yet elegant enough for guests.

West Lake poached fish is a specialty of Hangzhou, a lake resort in eastern China. The chefs there use only fresh-caught local fish, killed moments before cooking.

The gentle poaching technique used in this recipe retains the flavor and emphasizes the natural sweetness of fresh fish. You will achieve best results by using very fresh fillets of flounder or sole and not overcooking them.

Try to find a genuine Chinese red vinegar for making the sauce. Chinese rice-based vinegars are lighter and faintly sweeter than Western ones. If you must substitute red wine vinegar, use a good grade and taste the sauce to see whether you need to add a touch more sugar.

WHAT TO DRINK

With this family-style dinner serve a light red wine such as a Beaujolais or a California Gamay or, if you prefer white, California Chardonnay or a French Mâcon or Graves.

SHOPPING LIST AND STAPLES

4 very fresh fillets of flounder or sole (about ½ pound each)
½ skinless, boneless chicken breast
¼ pound fresh spinach
½ pound fresh snow peas
1 small bunch scallions
Fresh ginger
2 medium-size cloves garlic
1 large egg

8-ounce can water chestnuts
4 cups Chinese Chicken Stock (see page 13)
2 tablespoons corn, peanut, or vegetable oil
1 tablespoon Oriental sesame oil plus 1 tablespoon (optional)
4½ tablespoons light soy sauce
4 tablespoons Chinese red rice vinegar or 3 tablespoons Western red wine vinegar
1 cup uncooked rice
1 tablespoon plus 5½ teaspoons cornstarch
3 tablespoons sugar
Salt
Freshly ground white pepper (optional)
3 tablespoons plus 1 teaspoon dry sherry

UTENSILS

Food processor or blender
Wok or small saucepan (for fish)
Dutch oven with cover
2 large saucepans
Medium-size saucepan with cover (for rice)
2 small bowls
Metal colander
Measuring cups and spoons
Chinese cleaver or chef's knife
Paring knife
Wooden spoon
Wide, slotted metal spatula
Rubber spatula

1. Follow general rice recipe on page 12, steps 1 and 2.
2. Bring water to a boil for soup recipe and poached fish recipe, each step 1.
3. Shred scallion, if using, slice fresh ginger, and lightly crush and peel garlic cloves for poached fish.
4. Follow soup recipe steps 2 through 4.
5. Follow poached fish recipe steps 2 through 4.
6. Follow soup recipe steps 5 through 7. Preheat oven to 200 degrees.
7. Follow general rice recipe step 3 and poached fish recipe step 5. Keep fish warm in oven.
8. Complete soup, steps 8 through 10, and keep warm.
9. Follow snow pea recipe steps 1 through 3.
10. Follow poached fish recipe step 8.
11. Follow snow pea recipe steps 4 and 5, and poached fish recipe step 9. Serve with rice.

RECIPES

Emerald Soup

¼ pound fresh spinach (2 cups packed)
½ skinless, boneless chicken breast
1 tablespoon plus 1½ teaspoons cornstarch
1 teaspoon dry sherry
3¼ cups Chinese Chicken Stock
1 large egg white
2 tablespoons water
Salt
Freshly ground white pepper (optional)

1. Bring 4 cups water to a boil in large heavy saucepan.
2. Wash spinach well in several changes of water until no sand remains. Drain in colander.
3. Add spinach to the boiling water and bring water back to a boil, uncovered. Boil 30 seconds and quickly drain spinach in colander. Rinse under cold running water.
4. Squeeze spinach to remove excess water and shred finely with cleaver or knife. There should be about ⅓ cup.
5. Cut chicken into 1-inch cubes. Place cubes in blender or food processor and add 1½ teaspoons cornstarch, sherry, ¼ cup chicken stock, and egg white. Blend until chicken is pureed. If using food processor, puree chicken cubes before adding remaining ingredients, then process just until well blended. Transfer mixture to bowl.
6. Combine remaining cornstarch and water in small bowl.
7. Bring the 3 cups chicken stock to a boil in the saucepan used for the spinach.
8. Stir in pureed chicken mixture over low heat until it is well dispersed and chicken turns white.
9. Stir cornstarch mixture thoroughly and slowly add it to the hot soup, stirring constantly to prevent lumping. Bring soup back to a boil and cook 30 seconds.
10. Add chopped spinach and season with salt and white pepper. Keep warm, uncovered, in oven. Serve in soup tureen or in individual bowls.

Poached Fish Fillets, West Lake Style

4 very fresh fillets of flounder or sole (about ½ pound each)
2 scallions, cut in half lengthwise
Four ⅛-inch slices fresh ginger plus 1 tablespoon minced
3 tablespoons dry sherry
2 medium-size cloves garlic, peeled and lightly crushed
3 tablespoons light soy sauce
4 tablespoons Chinese red rice vinegar, or 3 tablespoons Western red wine vinegar
3 tablespoons sugar, or to taste
¾ cup Chinese Chicken Stock
4 teaspoons cornstarch mixed with 2 tablespoons water
2 tablespoons corn, peanut, or vegetable oil
1 tablespoon sesame oil (optional)
1 small scallion, cut into 2-inch lengths and finely shredded for garnish (optional)

1. In Dutch oven, bring 3 quarts water to a boil. Wipe fish with damp paper towels.
2. Add scallions, sliced ginger, and 2 tablespoons sherry to boiling water. Combine garlic and minced ginger for sauce in small bowl or cup.
3. In another bowl, combine remaining sherry, soy sauce, vinegar, sugar, and chicken stock.
4. Stir to dissolve cornstarch and water in small bowl.
5. When liquid returns to a boil, add fish. Cover and remove from heat. Fillets should be done in 1 to 1½ minutes, depending on their thickness. When transparency disappears, test to see if fish flakes easily. Gently lift fillets out, one at a time, with wide slotted spatula. Drain well and arrange over serving platter.
6. In wok or small saucepan, heat the 2 tablespoons of cooking oil over medium heat. Add garlic and ginger, and fry 30 seconds. Discard garlic.
7. Add sherry-soy sauce mixture and bring to a boil over high heat.
8. Stir cornstarch mixture thoroughly and slowly add it to the sauce, stirring constantly to prevent lumping. Bring to a boil and simmer 30 seconds. Remove from heat and add sesame oil, if desired. Set aside.
9. Remove fish fillets from oven and pour off any liquid that may have accumulated around them. Pour sauce over fish and decorate with shredded scallion, if desired.

Fresh Snow Pea Salad

½ pound fresh snow peas
4 ounces canned water chestnuts, drained
1½ tablespoons light soy sauce
1 tablespoon sesame oil

1. Bring 1 quart water to a boil in large heavy saucepan.
2. Pinch off stem ends of snow peas and pull off strings.
3. Cut water chestnuts into ¼-inch round slices.
4. Add snow peas to the boiling water and cook 30 to 60 seconds. Quickly drain in colander and rinse under cold running water. Drain well and blot dry with paper towels.
5. Place snow peas and water chestnuts in serving bowl. Toss with soy sauce and sesame oil. Serve.

Barbara Tropp

A s you sample an authentic Chinese meal, you will become aware of the delicate balance between one flavor and another, one texture and another. This balance derives from the Chinese philosophy of the duality of life—the *yin* and the *yang*, complementary opposites of human life, such as male and female, passive and active, sweet and sour. Barbara Tropp, a China scholar turned Chinese cook, brings this classic Chinese view of harmony to her cooking.

A native of New Jersey, Barbara Tropp spent two years in Taiwan, where she learned about Chinese food. After she returned to America, she became so homesick for Chinese cooking that she taught herself how to prepare Chinese meals. She has learned to adapt Chinese techniques to the fresh ingredients available in Western markets. Knowing that for most cooks speed is essential, she has revamped some of the lengthier traditional recipes to suit the often hectic pace of American life. She believes in practicality and economy—good taste above fancy presentation or lengthy preparation—so her menus do not require a large supply of expensive tools or ingredients.

Barbara Tropp favors the robust dishes of North China and the spicy hot foods of Szechwan and Hunan in the West. Menu 1 combines noodles with spicy beef—a popular northern dish—and hot and sour Hunan carrots. Menu 2, starring shrimp and eggplant, is a spicy Hunanese blend of chili, ginger, garlic, and scallions, and Menu 3 is multiregional.

The brilliant colors of this dinner, ideal for a winter evening, look delectable on lovely white platters and plates. You may highlight the noodles with a sprig or two of coriander, and be sure to arrange the red peppers on top of the stir-fried beef.

Spicy Hunan Beef with Scallions and Sweet Red Peppers
Warm Chinese Noodles with Sesame Oil
Hot and Sour Hunan Carrots

Both the beef and the noodle recipes call for a common Chinese ingredient—sesame oil. This dark brown nutty oil—a pantry basic—is not for cooking but for seasoning. Buy only a Chinese or Japanese brand; the cold-pressed health food or Middle Eastern types will not do.

In the hot and sour Hunan carrots, red chilies provide the hot taste, vinegar the sour, while the sprinkling of sugar enhances the flavor without sweetening the dish.

For this menu, the first step is to marinate the beef in the morning. At cooking time, you use a common Chinese technique that "double cooks" an ingredient. You sear the beef quickly in hot oil, then stir fry the other ingredients. For the last few seconds of cooking, you return the beef strips to the pan and combine all the ingredients.

WHAT TO DRINK

This spicy menu calls for a light, fruity wine with a touch of sweetness, such as a California Chenin Blanc.

SHOPPING LIST AND STAPLES

1 pound round or flank steak, trimmed of fat and gristle
1½ pounds baby carrots
1 red bell pepper
2 bunches scallions
1½ tablespoons Chinese salted black beans
Fresh coriander or Italian parsley sprigs (optional)
Fresh ginger
5 cloves garlic
1½ tablespoons *hoisin* sauce
⅔ cup unsalted Chinese Chicken Stock (see page 13)
3 to 4 cups plus 3½ tablespoons corn or peanut oil
2 tablespoons plus ¾ teaspoon Oriental sesame oil
1½ tablespoons unseasoned Oriental rice vinegar
6 tablespoons light soy sauce
1 pound ¹⁄₁₆-inch-thin Chinese egg noodles, fresh or dried
6½ teaspoons cornstarch
2 tablespoons plus 1⅜ teaspoons sugar
Kosher salt
1¼ teaspoons dried red pepper flakes
3 tablespoons Chinese rice wine or dry sherry

UTENSILS

Wok with cover
 or Dutch oven (for frying beef)
 and 12-inch skillet (for completing beef; carrots)
Stockpot or kettle
2 large bowls
4 small bowls
Saucer
Metal colander (optional)
Measuring cups and spoons
Chinese cleaver or chef's knife
Paring knife
Metal wok spatula or large wooden spoon
Chinese mesh spoon or long-handled slotted metal spoon
 (if not using colander)
16-inch chopsticks or 2 long-handled wooden spoons
Vegetable peeler
Deep-fat thermometer

START-TO-FINISH STEPS

In the morning: Follow Hunan beef recipe steps 1 and 2.
1. Follow warm Chinese noodles recipe step 1. While water comes to a boil, follow Hunan beef recipe steps 3 through 5.
2. Prepare carrots for Hunan carrots recipe step 1.
3. Wipe out wok. Follow Hunan beef recipe step 6.
4. Follow Hunan carrots recipe steps 2 through 4.
5. Follow Hunan beef recipe steps 7 through 12.
6. Follow Hunan carrots recipe steps 5 through 7.
7. Follow warm Chinese noodles recipe steps 2 and 3.
8. Follow Hunan carrots recipe step 8 and noodles recipe steps 4 through 6.
9. Remove beef and carrots from oven, and serve with warm noodles.

RECIPES

Spicy Hunan Beef with Scallions and Sweet Red Peppers

1 pound round or flank steak, trimmed of fat and gristle

The marinade:
2 tablespoons light soy sauce
4 teaspoons cornstarch
1 teaspoon sugar
1 tablespoon corn or peanut oil

The sauce:
3 tablespoons Chinese rice wine or dry sherry
2 tablespoons light soy sauce
2 tablespoons sugar
1½ tablespoons *hoisin* sauce
¾ teaspoon sesame oil

8 whole scallions
1 red bell pepper, cored, seeded, and cut into thin strips
2 to 3 teaspoons finely minced garlic (about 3 cloves)
2 to 3 teaspoons finely minced fresh ginger
½ to ¾ teaspoon dried red pepper flakes
3 to 4 cups corn or peanut oil
⅛ teaspoon kosher salt
⅛ teaspoon sugar

1. Prepare beef and marinade. Holding cleaver or knife at angle, cut beef against grain into long strips about ⅛ inch thick and ½ inch wide. Cut strips crosswise into 2-inch lengths.

2. Using fork, blend marinade ingredients in large bowl until smooth. Add beef and toss well to coat each slice. Seal and refrigerate. Remove 1 hour before preparation.

3. In small bowl stir to combine sauce ingredients.

4. Trim wilted tops and root ends from scallions. Cut on sharp diagonal into thin ovals about 1 inch long.

5. Core and seed pepper. Cut lengthwise into thinnest possible strips.

6. Combine garlic, ginger, and dried red pepper flakes in another small bowl.

7. Heat wok or Dutch oven over high heat until hot enough to evaporate a bead of water on contact. Add oil and heat to 350 degrees on deep-fat thermometer, or until a slice of beef bubbles very slowly when added. While oil is heating, drain beef in metal colander nested in large bowl.

8. Stir beef once more to coat the slices, then gently slide them into the oil. Carefully stir to separate beef slices and fry 15 seconds, just until beef is slightly gray.

9. Using pot holders, immediately pour beef and hot oil into metal colander. Or, working very fast, you may use a Chinese mesh spoon or long-handled slotted metal spoon to scoop out the beef, then drain on paper towels. Turn off heat and allow oil to cool before pouring it off. Reserve.

10. Wipe out wok, leaving thin film of oil. Heat wok or heavy skillet over high heat until a bead of water sizzles on contact. Add 2 tablespoons of the hot oil and swirl to coat pan. Reduce heat to medium. Add garlic, ginger, and pepper flakes, and stir about 10 seconds, adjusting heat so they do not brown.

11. Add red pepper strips and stir briskly to glaze them. Sprinkle with salt and sugar, then toss to combine, about 10 seconds in all. Drizzle in a bit more oil, if neccessary, to prevent sticking. Lower heat if peppers begin to scorch.

12. Stir sauce mixture, then add to pan, stirring to combine. Raise heat slightly to bring mixture to the bubbling point. Add beef and toss briskly to coat with sauce, about 5 seconds. Add scallions and toss briskly to combine and glaze with sauce, about 5 seconds. Do not let scallions wilt. Place in serving dish and keep warm in preheated 200-degree oven.

Warm Chinese Noodles with Sesame Oil

1 pound ¹⁄₁₆-inch-thin Chinese egg noodles, fresh or dried
2 teaspoons kosher salt

2 tablespoons sesame oil
Fresh coriander or Italian parsley for garnish (optional)

1. Bring 4 quarts unsalted water to a rolling boil in stockpot or kettle.

2. If using fresh noodles, fluff them and add to pot.

3. Using chopsticks or 2 long-handled wooden spoons, swish noodles gently back and forth several times to separate strands. Cook until a single strand tastes cooked but still firm to the bite.

4. Drain immediately in metal colander.

5. Return drained noodles to pot, combine with salt and sesame oil, and toss well to coat each strand.

6. Turn onto heated serving platter and garnish with fresh coriander or Italian parsley sprigs, if desired. Serve.

Hot and Sour Hunan Carrots

1½ pounds baby carrots
1½ tablespoons salted black beans, coarsely chopped
2½ teaspoons finely minced garlic (about 2 cloves)
2½ teaspoons finely minced fresh ginger
½ teaspoon dried red pepper flakes

The sauce:
½ cup unsalted Chinese Chicken Stock
2 tablespoons light soy sauce
1½ tablespoons unseasoned Oriental rice vinegar
¼ teaspoon sugar

2½ teaspoons cornstarch
1½ tablespoons Chinese Chicken Stock
2½ tablespoons corn or peanut oil

1. Peel and roll cut carrots (see page 10). There should be about 4 cups.

2. Combine black beans, garlic, ginger, and red pepper flakes in saucer.

3. Combine sauce ingredients in small bowl, stirring to dissolve sugar.

4. Blend cornstarch and broth until smooth. Set aside.

5. Heat wok or heavy skillet over high heat until hot enough to evaporate a bead of water on contact. Add oil, swirling to coat pan, then reduce heat to medium-high. Add black bean mixture and stir gently until fully fragrant, about 10 seconds.

6. Add carrots and toss briskly to combine and glaze each nugget with oil, drizzling in a bit more oil from side of pan, if necessary, to prevent sticking. Continue to toss until carrots feel hot to the touch, about 1 minute.

7. Stir sauce, then add to pan. Toss to combine it with the carrots, then raise heat to bring liquids to a simmer. Level the carrots, adjust heat to maintain a steady simmer, then cover pan. Cook 3 to 4 minutes, until carrots are tender-crisp and still a bit underdone. Taste sauce and adjust with an extra splash of vinegar or a dash of sugar.

8. Stir cornstarch and chicken broth mixture quickly to recombine, then add to pan. Stir until glossy and slightly thick, about 10 seconds. Remove to heated serving bowl and keep warm in preheated 200-degree oven.

Hoisin-Explosion Shrimp
Home-Style Spicy Eggplant
Spicy Cold Noodles with Sesame Sauce and Toasted Sesame Seeds

Hoisin-explosion shrimp are fresh shrimp cooked in the shell with *hoisin* sauce and wine. The "explosion" comes during the stir fry, when the alcohol evaporates and the sauce bubbles on contact with hot metal, causing the fragrances and flavors of the shellfish, spices, and wine to reach their peak. This is a home-style meal,

Though both the shrimp and eggplant are peppery to the taste, they provide pleasing contrasts in texture and color, which you can carry out in your table setting.

spicy but well-balanced in taste. The combination of shrimp and eggplant, soy sauce and vinegar, garlic and scallion unifies the meal and gives it a Hunanese character.

Most shrimp marketed today as fresh have been previously frozen and then thawed out in the fish market, but if you can buy truly fresh shrimp from a reliable fish store, do so. Otherwise look for a firm flesh, an intact shell, and a clean smell. The color of the shell is not an indication of freshness; it varies depending on locality and may be gray or pink.

Cooking shrimp in the shell is a favorite Chinese method

because the shell protects the tender shrimp and keeps it from drying out. Before you cook the shrimp, devein it as directed in the recipe and shown in the diagram, being careful not to detach the shell. You and your guests will find it easy to shell the shrimp once the shell has been cut.

Oriental eggplants—either Japanese or Chinese—are smaller and sweeter than the Western ones, and their skins are edible. If these varieties are not available, choose small Western eggplants with smooth, unblemished skins, but do not peel them.

The spicy cold noodles, tossed with a piquant sesame sauce and garnished with toasted sesame seeds, are especially good tasting and fun to eat. Fresh Chinese egg noodles are delicious, but if they are not available, select an Italian or Spanish dried egg noodle rather than a Chinese dried noodle.

Chinese black vinegar—used here to season the eggplant—is difficult to find. The best brand, according to Barbara Tropp, is Narcissus. Two readily available substitutes are Italian balsamic vinegar or California barengo vinegar, which you should be able to buy in any specialty food store.

Fresh coriander has a very pungent smell, unpleasant to some people, delightful to others. If you or your family and guests do not care for it, omit it and use Italian parsley instead.

WHAT TO DRINK

Chilled white wine is the appropriate drink to accompany this menu. Choose a California Sauvignon Blanc or Fumé Blanc for roundness and relative fullness. The cook also recommends a full-flavored Gewürztraminer from California or, if you prefer, Japanese beer.

SHOPPING LIST AND STAPLES

1½ pounds large fresh shrimp in the shell (15 to 20 shrimp)
2 pounds firm young eggplant, preferably long slender Oriental or small Italian variety
1 bunch scallions
1 bunch fresh coriander (optional)
Fresh ginger

10 cloves garlic
2 tablespoons *hoisin* sauce
6 tablespoons Chinese sesame paste
½ cup plus 6 tablespoons corn or peanut oil
5 tablespoons plus 1¼ teaspoons Oriental sesame oil
2 tablespoons sesame chili oil
2 tablespoons unseasoned Oriental rice vinegar
2 teaspoons plus dash Chinese black or balsamic vinegar
8 tablespoons light soy sauce
¾ pound ¹⁄₁₆-inch-thin Chinese egg noodles, preferably fresh
3 tablespoons plus 2 teaspoons sugar
2 tablespoons plus 1 teaspoon brown sugar
1¼ teaspoons dried red pepper flakes
2 tablespoons sesame seeds
2 tablespoons Chinese rice wine or dry sherry

UTENSILS

Food processor or blender
Wok with cover
 or 12-inch skillet with cover (for shrimp; eggplant)
Stockpot
 or Dutch oven (for noodles)
Small skillet
3 medium-size bowls
2 small bowls
3 small plates
Metal colander
Measuring cups and spoons
Chinese cleaver or chef's knife
Paring knife
Metal wok spatula or wooden spoon
16-inch chopsticks or 2 long-handled wooden spoons
Small scissors, preferably embroidery type

START-TO-FINISH STEPS

1. Follow spicy cold noodles recipe step 1 and set aside.
2. Follow eggplant recipe step 1.
3. Follow shrimp recipe steps 1 and 2.
4. Trim scallions for shrimp recipe step 3; trim and slice scallions for eggplant recipe step 2.
5. Follow spicy cold noodles recipe steps 2 and 3.
6. Follow eggplant recipe steps 3 and 4.
7. Follow cold noodles recipe steps 4 through 8.
8. Follow eggplant recipe steps 5 through 8 and shrimp recipe step 4.
9. Wipe out wok. Complete shrimp, steps 5 through 8.
10. Complete eggplant recipe step 9 and cold noodles recipe step 9, and serve with shrimp.

RECIPES

Hoisin-Explosion Shrimp

1½ pounds large fresh shrimp in the shell (15 to 20 shrimp)
2 scallions

1 tablespoon finely minced garlic (about 3 cloves)
½ to ¾ teaspoon dried red pepper flakes (optional)

The sauce:
2 tablespoons sugar
2 tablespoons *hoisin* sauce
2 tablespoons Chinese rice wine or dry sherry
2 tablespoons light soy sauce
½ teaspoon sesame oil
5 to 6 tablespoons corn or peanut oil
Fresh coriander sprigs for garnish (optional)

1. Using your fingers, pinch off legs of shrimp, several at a time, then bend back and snap off sharp, beaklike piece of shell just above tail. Using scissors with straight, thin blades, cut through shell along back of each shrimp all the way to the tail, taking care to expose black digestive vein. Extract black vein with point of scissors. Be careful not to loosen shell.

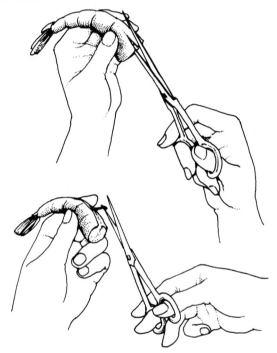

2. Put shrimp in colander, rinse briefly with cool water, then dry with paper towels. Remove to medium-size bowl and set aside.
3. Trim wilted green tops and roots from scallions. Cut scallions in half crosswise. Firmly grasp the pieces together and cut crosswise into ⅛-inch rings. Put aside ½ tablespoon for garnish if you are not using coriander. Put remaining scallion rings, garlic, and red pepper flakes side by side on small plate.
4. Stir to combine sauce ingredients in small bowl.
5. Heat wok or large heavy skillet over high heat until hot enough to evaporate a bead of water on contact. Add 5 tablespoons cooking oil, swirling to coat pan, then reduce heat to medium-high. Add garlic and stir so that it foams without browning. Add red pepper flakes and stir to combine. Then add scallion rings, again tossing several times to combine.
6. Add shrimp. Toss briskly 1 to 1½ minutes, until shrimp

turn pink and shells are evenly glazed with oil. Adjust heat so shrimp sizzle without scorching. Drizzle in more oil, if necessary, to keep shrimp and seasoning from sticking.

7. Stir sauce briefly to recombine, then add to pan. Raise heat to "explode" its fragrance (it will hiss and smell invitingly of wine), then toss briskly to combine. Toss until shrimp are evenly coated and sauce is slightly thick, about 10 seconds, then turn off heat.

8. Immediately transfer mixture to heated serving platter. Garnish with fresh coriander, if desired, or the reserved scallion rings.

Home-Style Spicy Eggplant

2 pounds firm, young eggplant, preferably long slender Oriental or small Italian variety
2 scallions
5 to 6 teaspoons finely minced garlic (about 5 to 7 cloves)
4 teaspoons finely minced fresh ginger
½ teaspoon dried red pepper flakes

The sauce:
⅔ cup water
3 tablespoons light soy sauce
2 tablespoons plus 1 teaspoon brown sugar
2 teaspoons Chinese black or balsamic vinegar

½ cup corn or peanut oil
Dash black or balsamic vinegar
¾ teaspoon Oriental sesame oil

1. Trim stem ends and brown base of eggplant, then roll cut (see page 10). If using Western eggplant, cut into pieces about 1¼ inches long, 1 inch wide, and 1 inch thick. There should be about 8 cups. Put in medium-size bowl and set aside.

2. Trim wilted green tops and roots from scallions and cut scallions crosswise in half. Firmly grasp the pieces together and cut them crosswise into ¼-inch rings. There should be about ⅓ cup. Reserve 2 teaspoons green and white rings for garnish.

3. Put remaining scallion rings, garlic, ginger, and pepper flakes side by side on small plate.

4. Stir to combine sauce ingredients.

5. Heat wok or large heavy skillet over high heat until hot enough to evaporate a bead of water on contact. Add cooking oil, swirling to coat pan, then reduce heat to medium-high. Add scallion rings, garlic, and ginger. Stir to disperse them in the oil, adjusting heat so mixture foams without browning. Add pepper flakes. Stir gently about 10 seconds.

6. Add eggplant, tossing pieces to glaze them and pressing them gently against side of pan to encourage browning. Adjust heat so eggplant sizzles gently without scorching. As pan becomes dry, drizzle in another tablespoon of oil from the side. Continue tossing eggplant and pressing it against pan 3 to 4 minutes, until eggplant is brown-edged and a bit soft.

7. Briefly stir sauce ingredients and add them to pan. Toss gently to combine, then raise heat to bring liquids to a simmer. Cover tightly and adjust heat to maintain a lively

simmer. Cook about 3 minutes, until liquids are absorbed, shaking pan to prevent eggplant from sticking.

8. Remove cover and toss eggplant. Add dash vinegar, sprinkle with sesame oil, then toss to combine.

9. Turn into serving dish, cover, and keep warm. Serve garnished with a sprinkling of the reserved scallion rings.

Spicy Cold Noodles with Sesame Sauce and Toasted Sesame Seeds

The sauce:
6 tablespoons sesame paste, drained of oil
5 tablespoons sesame oil
3 tablespoons light soy sauce
2 tablespoons sesame chili oil
2 tablespoons unseasoned Oriental rice vinegar
1 tablespoon plus 2 teaspoons sugar
2 to 3 tablespoons finely chopped fresh coriander leaves and upper stems (optional)
4 tablespoons water, approximately

2 tablespoons sesame seeds
¾ pound 1/16-inch-thin Chinese egg noodles, preferably fresh

1. In food processor fitted with metal blade or in blender, combine sauce ingredients until smooth. Add enough water so that mixture will fall from a spoon in wide, silky ribbons. Adjust seasoning to taste. Transfer mixture to bowl and seal airtight. Set aside at room temperature. (This can be made several hours in advance or refrigerated overnight. Bring to room temperature before using.)

2. Bring 4 quarts unsalted water to a rolling boil in stockpot or Dutch oven.

3. Toast sesame seeds in small, heavy skillet over medium heat, stirring until golden, about 3 minutes. Remove to a plate to cool.

4. If using fresh noodles, fluff them to separate strands before adding to pot. Using wooden chopsticks or 2 long-handled wooden spoons, swish noodles gently back and forth several times to separate strands. Cook fresh noodles 1 to 2 minutes, until a single strand tastes cooked but still firm to the bite. Cook 4 to 8 minutes more if using dried noodles.

5. Drain immediately in colander and flush with cold running water until noodles are thoroughly chilled, tossing them gently to chill them quickly and evenly. Shake well to remove excess water.

6. Dry pot and return noodles to it.

7. Stir sauce. If it thickened when refrigerated, blend in a bit more water to achieve ribbony consistency. Do not thin sauce too much; it should cling to the noodles.

8. Pour half the sauce over the noodles and with your hands or wooden spoons toss gently to coat and separate each strand. Do not break the noodles (which to the Chinese are emblematic of long life). Pour remaining sauce into small bowl and serve separately.

9. Just before serving, toss noodles to redistribute sauce. Serve on individual plates or in shallow pasta bowls and sprinkle toasted sesame seeds on top.

Steamed Spicy Fish with Black Mushrooms and Ham
Temple Fried Rice
Cold-Tossed Watercress with Sesame Seeds

A long, oval platter makes the best setting for a whole steamed fish. Use a broad server, which both cuts and lifts, for slicing and serving the fish. Serve the watercress on individual plates, if you wish.

Ideal for a summer evening, this elegant meal of steamed fish, fried rice, and watercress salad depends (as do all the menus in this book) on fresh ingredients simply prepared. When you buy the fish, choose a whole one with bright red gills and glassy black eyes, as these are signs of freshness. Be sure to have the scales, fins, gills, and guts—including the air bladder—removed, but ask the fishmonger to leave the head and tail intact. If you cannot find a small, whole fish, use a two-pound section of a larger fish and have it cut in half lengthwise, through the backbone, so that you can lay it in the steamer skin side up as if it were two fish. Score the skin side only (see diagram).

Temple fried rice is a vegetarian dish, common to Buddhist temple kitchens. Since Buddhists are vegetarians who omit strongly flavored foods from their diets, this dish omits the meat, onions, and scallions that are typical ingredients in fried rice. Its unusual savoriness comes from celery heart, carrots, pine nuts, and eggs.

The watercress salad, briefly cooked, is a northern dish. Buy the crispest watercress you can find: good produce markets keep it standing in cold water or on shaved ice.

WHAT TO DRINK

Although Chinese foods usually call for a slightly sweet wine, a drier white would taste good here because of the savory rice and egg dish. Try either an Alsatian Sylvaner or a crisp Soave from Italy.

SHOPPING LIST AND STAPLES

3 pounds fresh whole fish (pompano, sea bass, porgy, flounder, or wall-eye), cleaned and gutted, with head and tail left on
1 ounce Smithfield ham or prosciutto, cut into paper-thin slices
4 bunches fresh watercress (about 1½ pounds)
2 medium-size carrots
1 bunch celery
1 red bell pepper (optional)
1 large scallion
6 to 8 Chinese dried black mushrooms
Fresh ginger
2 cloves garlic
3 large eggs
4½ to 5 tablespoons corn or peanut oil
7 teaspoons Oriental sesame oil

2 teaspoons unseasoned Oriental rice vinegar
4 tablespoons plus 2 teaspoons light soy sauce
1 cup uncooked rice
4¼ teaspoons sugar
Kosher salt
Dried red pepper flakes
4 ounces pine nuts
2 teaspoons raw or black sesame seeds
2 tablespoons plus 2 teaspoons Chinese rice wine or dry sherry

UTENSILS

Wok
    or 12-inch skillet (for completing rice)
Large stockpot
    or Dutch oven (for watercress)
Small heavy skillet
Medium-size saucepan with cover (for rice)
Fish steamer or large sauté pan with lid
Heatproof oval platter with sloping sides
Small flat plate
Large mixing bowl
4 small bowls
2 saucers
Metal colander
1-inch metal trivet (for steaming, if using sauté pan)
Measuring cups and spoons
Chinese cleaver or chef's knife
Metal wok spatula or long-handled wooden spoon
2 wooden spoons
Small whisk
Vegetable peeler
Scissors

START-TO-FINISH STEPS

1. For fried rice recipe, follow general rice recipe on page 12, steps 1 and 2.
2. Bring to a boil 1 cup water. Follow fish recipe step 1.
3. Follow fish recipe steps 2 and 3, and fried rice recipe steps 1 and 2.
4. Follow watercress recipe steps 2 and 3.
5. Follow watercress recipe step 4 and fried rice recipe step 3.
6. Follow watercress recipe steps 5 through 7.
7. Follow fish recipe steps 4 through 8.
8. Follow watercress recipe step 8.

9. Follow fish recipe steps 9 through 11.

10. Complete general rice recipe step 3.

11. Follow fish recipe step 12. While fish is steaming, beat eggs for fried rice recipe and follow step 4. Remove cover on cooked rice, step 4.

12. Follow fried rice recipe steps 5 through 8 and watercress recipe step 9.

13. Complete fried rice recipe steps 9 and 10, and fish recipe step 10. Serve at once.

RECIPES

Steamed Spicy Fish with Black Mushrooms and Ham

6 to 8 Chinese dried black mushrooms

3 pounds fresh whole fish (pompano, sea bass, porgy, flounder, or wall-eye), cleaned and gutted, with head and tail left on

1 ounce Smithfield ham or prosciutto, cut into paper-thin slices

2 teaspoons kosher salt

¼ teaspoon sugar

2 tablespoons Chinese rice wine or dry sherry

2 tablespoons light soy sauce

2 teaspoons sesame oil

2 teaspoons garlic, finely minced (about 2 cloves)

1½ teaspoons finely minced fresh ginger

½ teaspoon dried red pepper flakes

3 tablespoons thinly sliced scallion

1. Cover mushrooms with boiling water and allow to soak 20 to 30 minutes.

2. Trim fat from ham or prosciutto. Mince fat and reserve about 1 scant tablespoon. Cut ham into pieces about 1 inch square.

3. Rinse fish clean with water, inside and out. Shake to remove excess water, then pat fish dry inside and out with paper towels.

4. Holding cleaver or knife at a 45-degree angle, score fish at 1-inch intervals from neck to tail on both sides. Follow natural curve of collar and extend each cut from dorsal to ventral sides of fish (that is, from top to belly), cutting down nearly to the bone.

5. Sprinkle salt evenly over outside and inside of fish. Gently rub salt in score marks.

6. Put fish on heatproof oval platter about 1 inch smaller than fish steamer or large sauté pan. (If using bamboo steamer, see page 13.)

7. In small bowl, stir to combine wine, soy sauce, sesame oil, and sugar. Add garlic and ginger, and stir to blend. Pour mixture over fish.

8. In another bowl, combine reserved minced fat, red pepper flakes, and scallion rings. Sprinkle over fish.

9. Drain mushrooms and, using scissors, snip off stems and cut caps in half. Rinse caps under cold running water to dislodge any sand.

10. Neatly arrange ham and mushrooms along curve of fish. Seal platter with plastic wrap.

11. Bring hot water to a gushing boil in covered steamer or large sauté pan. The water should not touch platter on which fish will steam.

12. Remove plastic wrap and put platter with fish on steaming rack or trivet. Wait until steam surges around fish, then reduce heat to medium-high and cover pan. Steam fish 10 to 15 minutes, depending on thickness of fish, or until flesh at base of score marks is white and firm. Do not overcook, as the fish will continue to cook from its own heat when it is removed from burner.

13. If fish was cooked in steamer, bring steamer directly to the table on a tray. Otherwise, lift out serving plate and place on serving trivet at the table.

Temple Fried Rice

2 medium-size carrots, peeled and trimmed

1 celery heart, plus several trimmed inner stalks

½ cup pine nuts

4½ to 5 tablespoons corn or peanut oil

3 large eggs, beaten

1 teaspoon Kosher salt or 2 tablespoons light soy sauce

2 teaspoons Chinese rice wine or dry sherry

3½ cups cooked rice, at room temperature

1. Cut carrots lengthwise in half. Lay halves flat and cut lengthwise in half again. Firmly grasp the pieces together and cut crosswise into small, fan-shaped pieces, about ⅛ inch thick. Cut enough to measure about ⅔ cup. Put in small bowl.

2. Cut celery heart, leaves and all, into thin slices. Cut celery stalks lengthwise into fourths. Firmly grasp the pieces together in tight bunch and cut them crosswise into thin arcs. Measure out about ½ cup and reserve in small bowl.

3. Toast pine nuts in small heavy skillet until fragrant and lightly golden, about 2 to 3 minutes on medium to medium-high heat. Shake pan so nuts do not brown. Pour nuts into saucer and set aside.

4. Heat wok or skillet over high heat until hot enough to evaporate a bead of water on contact. Add 2½ tablespoons oil and swirl to coat pan. Reduce heat to medium-high and add beaten eggs to pan. They should puff and bubble immediately. Pause 2 to 3 seconds until a film of cooked egg sets on bottom, then tip pan toward you and with wooden spoon push cooked egg away. Pause about 2 seconds for a new film to set on bottom, then push it to far side of pan. Continue until there is no more flowing egg. Turn out soft mass onto flat plate and slice into dime-size bits or slivers. The egg should be moist, yellow, and loosely set. It will cook to doneness when combined with rice.

5. Heat wok or heavy skillet over medium-high heat until hot enough to evaporate a bead of water on contact. Add 2 tablespoons oil, swirling to coat bottom. When oil is hot, add carrots and stir fry briskly, about 15 seconds, in order to glaze pieces with oil and heat them through.

6. Add celery and toss briskly about 10 seconds. Scatter wine (or sherry) into pan and toss quickly just to mix.

7. Immediately add rice and toss briskly to combine. Lower heat if rice begins to scorch and drizzle in a bit more oil from the side if rice is sticking badly (it does tend to stick a little bit). Continue tossing until rice is heated through.

8. Sprinkle salt or soy sauce over rice and toss briskly to blend. Then taste, adding more seasoning if needed.

9. Return eggs to pan and toss gently 10 seconds just to combine and heat through.

10. Put rice in serving bowl and scatter in pine nuts. Toss gently to combine.

Cold-Tossed Watercress with Sesame Seeds

4 bunches fresh watercress (about 1½ pounds)

2 teaspoons raw or black sesame seeds
4 teaspoons sugar
5 teaspoons sesame oil
2 teaspoons light soy sauce
2 teaspoons unseasoned Oriental rice vinegar

1. Bring 4 quarts unsalted water to a boil in large stockpot or Dutch oven.

2. Cut watercress above band that joins each bunch and discard stems. Discard any wilted or discolored pieces from leafy tops.

3. Fill large mixing bowl with cold water and add watercress. Pump up and down with your hand to dislodge any dirt. Drain in colander, then shake off excess water. Dry bowl.

4. If using raw sesame seeds, toast them in small heavy skillet over medium heat, stirring until golden, about 3 minutes. Put seeds aside on saucer to cool. Black seeds do not require toasting.

5. Add watercress to the boiling water, pushing leaves beneath surface with spatula. Blanch 20 seconds, then drain immediately in colander and flush with cold running water until chilled.

6. Using your hands, press down gently but firmly to remove excess water, then sandwich watercress between two triple thicknesses of paper towels and pat dry.

7. Transfer watercress to the large mixing bowl. Fluff mass with your fingers and gently separate leaves.

8. Whisk sugar, sesame oil, soy sauce, and rice vinegar in small bowl, stirring briskly to thicken mixture. Taste and adjust with a bit more sugar, if desired. Pour sauce over watercress and with your fingers toss well to coat leaves. Cover with plastic wrap and chill.

9. Just before serving, toss watercress to redistribute seasonings. Mound on plate or in shallow bowl of contrasting color, then sprinkle sesame seeds on top.

ADDED TOUCH

For a fruit compote that will satisfyingly end this meal, peel and section one large grapefruit and four medium oranges, reserving their juice. Arrange the fruit in 4 serving dishes and drizzle the juice over them. Serve plain, or top with blueberries or whole strawberries, if in season. Sliced fresh kiwi fruit is also good, and you might combine it with lemon, lime, or tangerine sherbet.

Audrey and Calvin Lee

MENU 1 (Left)
Seafood Treasure Noodles
Shantung Chicken with Hot Hoisin Sauce

MENU 2
Lion's Head
Stir-Fried Cauliflower and Sweet Peppers
Rice

MENU 3
Corn Soup
Red-Cooked Duck
Asparagus Salad
Rice

Chinese cooks frequently combine the full range of Chinese regional cooking techniques—braising, poaching, steaming, deep frying, and stir frying—when preparing an entire meal, and often they use two or three techniques within a single recipe. Such diversity has long appealed to Calvin and Audrey Lee.

Mr. Lee's heritage and training—in a family-owned restaurant—are Cantonese, but he has enjoyed experimenting with all of China's regional dishes. Mrs. Lee emphasizes the importance of visual impact and urges you to take time to arrange the food carefully on the serving platter with such garnishes as toasted sesame seeds or chopped scallions. Together the Lees believe in the merits of each region's style of cooking, so they have borrowed from all to develop their own particular approach.

Each of their menus is suitable for serving either family or guests because they are all exceptionally attractive yet simple to prepare. In the Cantonese-style Menu 1, a medley of seafood rests on cooked noodles—a Chinese favorite often served as part of the main meal or between meals as a substantial snack. In Menu 2, the ingredients suggest the name of the dish, *lion's head:* meatballs represent the lion's head, the vegetable its mane. The duck in Menu 3 cooks in a savory sauce and arrives at the table with a pungent asparagus salad and delicate corn soup.

A noodle dish of stir-fried scallops, shrimp, and squid, if you wish, pairs beautifully with the richly colored chicken in hot hoisin sauce. Pass a bowl of sliced scallions so that guests can add more to the chicken.

Seafood Treasure Noodles
Shantung Chicken with Hot Hoisin Sauce

The focal point of this substantial meal is the stir-fried seafood on a bed of noodles, a dish that is a year-round Chinese favorite. Because of their length, noodles are symbols of longevity to the Chinese, who have invented endless variations on the noodle theme. Oriental noodles are made with eggs and wheat or rice flours, and come in a variety of shapes. Whether you buy fresh or dried Oriental noodles for this recipe, you must boil them first and then let them drain before stir frying them. For this recipe, you form the cooked noodles into four pancakes, then fry them on each side until they are crispy brown. You may use spaghetti or vermicelli instead.

A medley of fresh seafood—shrimp, scallops, and, if you wish, squid—are a sweet and flavorful topping for the noodles. You stir fry the seafood with broccoli, snow peas, water chestnuts, and straw mushrooms, then blend them with oyster sauce, which unifies the seafood flavors.

The sweet yet spicy chicken with *hoisin* sauce is an accent dish, a counterpoint to the sweet seafood. The *hoisin* sauce is sweet, and the dried red pepper flakes spicy hot.

WHAT TO DRINK

The cooks suggest a dry white wine with a medium body to accompany this menu—either a French Graves or a dry California Sauvignon Blanc, for example.

SHOPPING LIST AND STAPLES

1 pound skinless, boneless chicken breasts (about 2 whole breasts)
½ pound medium-size shrimp (about 8 to 10)
½ pound bay or sea scallops
1 small squid, cleaned (optional)
2 bunches broccoli (about 1½ pounds)
¼ pound fresh snow peas
2 bunches scallions
Fresh ginger
¼ cup Chinese Chicken Stock (see page 13)
15-ounce can straw mushrooms
8-ounce can water chestnuts
3 tablespoons oyster sauce
2 tablespoons *hoisin* sauce
8 tablespoons peanut oil
2 teaspoons Oriental sesame oil
1 tablespoon dark soy sauce

½ pound thin Chinese egg noodles or vermicelli
Salt
½ teaspoon dried red pepper flakes
4 teaspoons dry sherry

UTENSILS

Stockpot or kettle
Wok with cover
    or heavy 12-inch skillet with cover (for noodles; seafood; chicken)
3 medium-size bowls
Metal colander
Measuring cups and spoons
Chinese cleaver or chef's knife
Paring knife
Metal wok spatula or slotted metal spatula
2 wooden spoons

START-TO-FINISH STEPS

1. Bring 3 quarts water to a boil for noodles recipe step 1.
2. Follow Shantung chicken recipe steps 1 and 2.
3. Follow noodle recipe steps 2 through 8.
4. Preheat oven to 200 degrees and follow Shantung chicken recipe steps 3 through 7.
5. Wipe out pan. Follow noodles recipe steps 9 through 15. Remove chicken from oven and serve.

RECIPES

Seafood Treasure Noodles

½ pound thin Chinese egg noodles or vermicelli
1 bunch broccoli (about 1½ pounds)
¼ pound fresh snow peas
15-ounce can straw mushrooms
8-ounce can water chestnuts, drained
4 scallions
½ pound medium shrimp (about 8 to 10)
½ pound bay or sea scallops
1 small squid, cleaned (optional)
6 tablespoons peanut oil
Salt
2 quarter-size slices fresh ginger
2 teaspoons dry sherry

2 tablespoons water
3 tablespoons oyster sauce
2 teaspoons Oriental sesame oil

1. Bring stockpot or kettle of water to a boil over high heat.
2. Add noodles and cook 5 minutes, or until noodles are firm to the bite. Drain in colander and rinse under cold running water. Pat dry. Divide into 4 mounds.
3. Cut broccoli into flowerets 2 inches long. Peel stems so they are about ¼ inch thick. You should have 3 cups of flowerets. (Save stems and any leftover flowerets for another use.)
4. String snow peas and set aside in bowl. Drain straw mushrooms and add to the snow peas. Slice each water chestnut into ⅛-inch ovals and add to the vegetables.
5. Slice scallions, including the green, into ¼-inch lengths and put aside separately for garnish.
6. Peel shrimp. Using small sharp knife, slice halfway through back of each shrimp and remove black vein. Shrimp will curl prettily when cooked.
7. Rinse scallops. If using sea scallops, quarter each one. If using bay scallops, leave them whole.
8. If using squid, first hold head with one hand and body with the other, and firmly pull head from body sac. Next, take hold of quill-like piece located at top of body sac and remove it by pulling. Make sure you get all of it, as it may break into smaller pieces. Peel away the black-flecked skin and rinse squid. Cut away tentacles and leave whole. Slice body into ⅛-inch rings. (See diagrams below.)
9. Heat wok or large, heavy skillet over high heat. Add 2 tablespoons peanut oil and ¼ teaspoon salt, and stir to coat pan. When oil is quite hot, add the 4 mounds of noodles. Press down firmly on each mound with back of metal spatula to form 4 pancakes about ½ inch thick.
10. Pan fry the noodle pancakes 2 minutes, or until light brown and crusty. Turn pancakes and brown other side 2 minutes. Remove to serving platter lined with paper towels to drain; keep warm.
11. Wipe out pan with paper towels. Add 2 tablespoons peanut oil to pan and heat until almost smoking. Add ¼ teaspoon salt and ginger. Stir to distribute oil. Add shrimp and squid. Stir 1 minute. Add half the sherry and stir

briefly just until shrimp turn pink. Repeat process for scallops and cook until opaque. Remove scallops to bowl and discard ginger.
12. Wipe out pan with paper towels and reheat over high heat. Add 2 tablespoons peanut oil and ¼ teaspoon salt. When oil is almost smoking, add broccoli and stir 1 minute. Add snow peas, straw mushrooms, and water chestnuts, and cook, stirring, 1 minute. Add water, cover pan, and cook 2 minutes.
13. Uncover and return seafood to pan. Stir to mix with the vegetables. Add oyster sauce and stir to blend.
14. Remove pan from heat and stir in sesame oil.
15. Place equal portions of seafood mixture on each noodle pancake and serve immediately with garnish of chopped scallions on the side.

Shantung Chicken with Hot Hoisin Sauce

1 pound skinless, boneless chicken breasts (about 2 whole breasts)
2 tablespoons *hoisin* sauce
2 teaspoons dry sherry
1 tablespoon dark soy sauce
4 scallions
2 tablespoons peanut oil
½ teaspoon dried red pepper flakes
¼ cup Chinese Chicken Stock

1. Cut chicken into ½-inch squares.
2. Combine *hoisin* sauce, sherry, and soy sauce in mixing bowl. Add chicken and coat well with sauce. Let chicken marinate until ready to cook.
3. Slice scallions into ½-inch lengths. Set aside for garnish.
4. Heat wok or skillet over high heat. Add oil and red pepper flakes, and stir briefly to distribute oil in pan. When oil is almost smoking, carefully add chicken and marinade. Stir fry vigorously 1 minute.
5. Carefully add chicken stock and stir quickly to blend. Cover and cook 2 minutes.
6. Uncover and cook a few minutes more to reduce sauce slightly, stirring constantly.
7. Remove to serving dish and garnish with the scallions. Keep warm in preheated 200-degree oven.

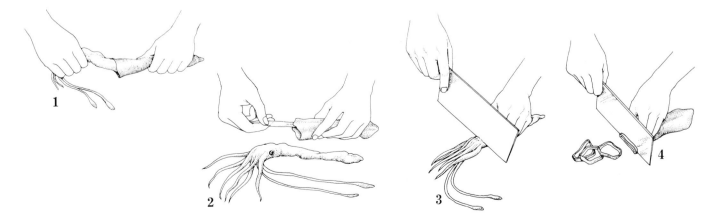

Lion's Head
Stir-Fried Cauliflower and Sweet Peppers
Rice

Heavy white pottery bowls make perfect serving pieces for this attractive but simple dinner. The braised meatballs mimic lions' heads, and the cooked spinach leaves are the manes. Cauliflower and red pepper add a color contrast.

The lion's head recipe exemplifies the Chinese delight in symbolism and the use of whimsical names. The original recipe calls for huge meatballs, but here the Lees have made them smaller in the interest of cooking speed and have substituted spinach for the more traditional Chinese cabbage.

Stir-fried cauliflower and slices of red pepper are lightly seasoned with fresh ginger, soy sauce, and sesame oil.

The Lees include their special method for treating rice. Washing and rinsing rice until the water runs clear is a ritual in Chinese kitchens, and is thought to tenderize rice and improve the taste.

WHAT TO DRINK

The cooks recommend an imported beer for this meal, and they prefer the dark and malty variety to light lagers. Several Mexican beers, some dark German beers, and some of the darker English ales would be ideal.

SHOPPING LIST AND STAPLES

1 pound ground pork
1½ pounds fresh spinach, or 2 ten-ounce packages frozen
1 small head cauliflower (about 1 pound)
1 large red pepper
1 bunch scallions
Fresh ginger
8-ounce can water chestnuts
1 egg
¾ cup Chinese Chicken Stock (see page 13) or canned broth
½ cup plus 2 tablespoons peanut oil
1 teaspoon Oriental sesame oil
3 tablespoons dark soy sauce
½ teaspoon light soy sauce
1 tablespoon plus 2 teaspoons cornstarch
1½ cups uncooked long-grain rice
½ teaspoon sugar
Salt
2 teaspoons dry sherry

UTENSILS

Food processor
Wok
　or heavy 12-inch skillet with cover (for cauliflower)
Dutch oven or flameproof casserole with cover

42

1½-quart saucepan with cover
Small platter
Large bowl
Small bowl
Metal colander
Measuring cups and spoons
Chinese cleaver or chef's knife
Paring knife
Slotted spoon
Wok spatula or 2 long-handled wooden spoons
Small cup

START-TO-FINISH STEPS

1. Follow rice recipe steps 1 and 2.
2. Follow lion's head recipe steps 1 and 2.
3. Follow rice recipe step 3 and lion's head recipe steps 3 through 7.
4. Preheat oven to 200 degrees. Follow stir-fried cauliflower recipe steps 1 and 2.
5. Complete lion's head recipe, steps 8 through 10.
6. Follow rice recipe step 4 and cauliflower recipe steps 3 through 6. Remove lion's head dish from oven and serve.

RECIPES

Lion's Head

1½ pounds fresh spinach, or 2 ten-ounce packages frozen
12 water chestnuts
1½-inch knob fresh ginger
4 scallions, trimmed
1 pound ground pork
1 egg
½ teaspoon sesame oil
2 teaspoons dry sherry
3 tablespoons dark soy sauce
1 tablespoon plus 2 teaspoons cornstarch
½ cup peanut oil
½ cup Chinese Chicken Stock or canned broth
½ teaspoon sugar

1. Wash spinach and trim off tough stems. Drain leaves well in colander. Pat dry with paper towels.
2. Using food processor fitted with steel blade or using a knife, mince water chestnuts. You should have about ½ cup. Peel and mince fresh ginger to measure about 2 tablespoons. Remove root ends and slice scallions into thin rounds. Combine water chestnuts, scallions, ginger, and ground meat in large bowl.
3. Beat egg in small bowl and add it to pork mixture along with sesame oil, sherry, and 1 tablespoon dark soy sauce. Sprinkle with 1 tablespoon cornstarch.
4. Blend mixture well and form into 16 meatballs about 1½ inches in diameter.
5. Heat peanut oil in Dutch oven or flameproof casserole until it is almost smoking. Add meatballs and brown thoroughly, about 6 to 8 minutes.

6. Meanwhile, combine chicken stock or broth, remaining 2 tablespoons dark soy sauce, and sugar in small cup.
7. When meatballs have browned, remove them with slotted spoon to platter and pour off oil. Add chicken stock mixture to Dutch oven or casserole and bring to a boil. Return meatballs to pot. Cover and regulate heat so that liquid bubbles steadily.
8. After meatballs have cooked 10 to 15 minutes, uncover and place spinach on top of meatballs. Replace lid. You may have to push lid down firmly at first to get all the spinach in pot. Raise heat and steam 3 to 5 minutes, or until done.
9. Remove spinach with slotted spoon and arrange on shallow serving dish. Arrange meatballs on top of spinach.
10. Bring leftover cooking liquid to a boil. Combine remaining 2 teaspoons cornstarch with 1 tablespoon water and add to sauce in pan. Stir vigorously for a moment or until thickened. Pour sauce over meatballs and spinach. Keep warm until ready to serve.

Stir-Fried Cauliflower and Sweet Peppers

1 small head cauliflower (about 1 pound)
1 large red pepper
2 quarter-size slices fresh ginger
¼ cup Chinese Chicken Stock
½ teaspoon light soy sauce
2 tablespoons peanut oil
½ teaspoon salt
½ teaspoon sesame oil

1. Cut cauliflower into flowerets approximately 1½ inches across. Discard green leaves. Core and remove seeds from pepper; slice lengthwise into ½-inch strips. Slice fresh ginger.
2. In measuring cup, combine chicken stock and light soy sauce.
3. Heat oil in wok or large heavy skillet until very hot. Maintain high heat throughout cooking process. Add salt and ginger. Stir 10 seconds.
4. Add cauliflower and pepper. Stir 1 minute.
5. Add chicken stock mixture and stir to coat vegetables. Cover pan and cook 2 to 5 minutes.
6. Remove pan from heat and stir in sesame oil. Serve immediately.

Rice

1½ cups long-grain rice
2¼ cups water

1. Wash rice by rubbing it between your hands in several changes of water to remove any excess starch.
2. Combine rice and water in 1½-quart saucepan. Bring to a boil over high heat. Continue to boil rice, uncovered, about 5 minutes, until virtually all visible water has evaporated, leaving bubbles and air holes on surface of rice.
3. Cover pan and simmer over very low heat 18 or 20 minutes.
4. Uncover and stir well to fluff rice before serving.

Corn Soup
Red-Cooked Duck
Asparagus Salad / Rice

O ne of the hallmarks of Shanghai or eastern-style cooking is the red-cooking method—a method involving the use of dark brown soy sauce in a liquid to

Corn soup, red-cooked duck, steamed rice, and an asparagus salad served on traditional Chinese dinnerware look at home in a dramatic table setting.

braise, or slow-cook, a meat until it is tender. The soy sauce is what gives the meat its reddish color. This technique adapts equally well to meat, poultry, and seafood, whether cooked whole or chopped into smaller portions. And the cooking broth, which you can strain and refrigerate for reuse, improves with age.

Normally this method requires several hours of cooking

time, but the quartered duck in this recipe cooks through quickly. The market for duck has grown rapidly in the past few years, and fresh ducks—as well as frozen—are increasingly available from meat markets and some supermarkets. To get a fresh duck, you may need to notify your meatman or butcher a couple of days in advance. If you buy a frozen duck, check the expiration date on the package.

The Lees call for a heavy cleaver for cutting off the wing tips and quartering the duck. A chef's knife will also do the work, or you can ask the butcher to quarter the duck when you buy it. At this meal you probably should give your guests the option of using a knife and fork instead of chopsticks, since picking meat off the bones with a pair of chopsticks requires a certain dexterity. However, this braised duck is so tender that the meat comes off the bone with little difficulty.

You can make the asparagus salad ahead and serve it either at room temperature or slightly chilled. The dressing, a Chinese version of a French vinaigrette, is particularly good with the rich-tasting duck. Always use fresh asparagus. If the season is past, however, you may substitute green beans. Cook them exactly as you would the asparagus and use the same dressing.

The creamy corn soup takes only minutes to prepare; flavored with chicken and ham, it is particularly delicious with chicken or duck.

WHAT TO DRINK

With this menu, try either a light red wine, such as a Beaujolais or a young Chianti, or a fuller-bodied wine, such as a California or Alsatian Gewürztraminer. The cooks do not recommend beer, but Calvin Lee's personal choice, rather than wine, is a single dry martini, served very cold.

4½-pound duck
¼ pound skinless, boneless chicken breast (about 1 small
    whole breast)
1 ounce slice Smithfield or Westphalian ham
24 asparagus spears (about 1½ pounds)
1 bunch scallions
1 egg
1 cup milk
1 cup Chinese Chicken Stock (see page 13)
2 teaspoons Oriental sesame oil
1 cup plus 1 tablespoon dark soy sauce
1 cup light soy sauce
1 teaspoon Chinese rice wine vinegar
1 cup uncooked rice
1 teaspoon cornstarch
¼ cup plus 1½ teaspoons sugar
10-ounce package frozen corn
Salt
2 star anise
1 teaspoon raw sesame seeds

UTENSILS

Food processor
Stockpot or kettle with cover
Wok or 5-quart Dutch oven (for duck)
7-inch skillet with cover
2 medium-size saucepans, 1 with cover (for rice)
2 medium-size bowls
2 small bowls
Metal colander
Measuring cups and spoons
Heavy Chinese cleaver or chef's knife
Paring knife
2 wooden spoons
Whisk
Soup ladle
Fat separator (optional)

START-TO-FINISH STEPS

1. Cut scallions into 1-inch thick lengths and follow red-cooked duck recipe steps 1 through 4.
2. While duck is cooking, follow general rice recipe on page 12, steps 1 and 2.

3. Follow corn soup recipe steps 1 through 3.
4. Follow duck recipe step 5 and general rice recipe step 3.
5. Follow soup recipe step 4 and asparagus recipe steps 1 through 5.
6. Follow soup recipe steps 5 and 6 and red-cooked duck recipe steps 6 and 7.
7. Complete asparagus recipe, steps 6 and 7, rice recipe, step 4, and serve.

RECIPES

Corn Soup

10-ounce package frozen corn
1 cup milk
¼ pound skinless, boneless chicken breast
¼ cup plus 3 tablespoons water
1 cup Chinese Chicken Stock
½ teaspoon salt
½ teaspoon sugar
⅛-inch slice Smithfield or Westphalian ham
1 teaspoon cornstarch
1 egg white

1. In medium-size saucepan of boiling water to cover, cook package of corn 5 minutes. Remove from heat and drain pan. Open package, return contents to pan, and simmer with 1 cup milk until tender.
2. In food processor fitted with steel blade, puree chicken. Or mince chicken, first using sharp edge and then using blunt edge of knife. Combine with ¼ cup water in small bowl. Set aside.
3. Combine chicken stock, salt, and sugar with the creamed corn in saucepan and bring to a boil over medium heat, stirring occasionally.
4. Mince ham and add to soup along with minced chicken mixture. Simmer, stirring, 2 minutes.
5. Mix cornstarch with 3 tablespoons water in measuring cup. Slowly add cornstarch mixture to soup. Cook, stirring, to thicken slightly. Remove from heat.
6. Beat egg white in medium-size bowl with fork or whisk until light and foamy. Stirring constantly, drizzle egg white into hot soup to form long, thin threads. Keep warm until ready to serve, but do not allow to boil.

Red-Cooked Duck

1 cup dark soy sauce
1 cup light soy sauce

1 cup water
¼ cup sugar
2 star anise (16 sections)
4½-pound duckling
4 scallions, cut into thirds

1. In wok or 5-quart Dutch oven, combine all ingredients except duck and scallions, and bring to a boil.

2. Remove any excess fat from cavity of duck. Trim off neck skin. Chop off wing tips and save with neck and gizzards for future use. With heavy cleaver, quarter duck: Place duck breast side up and cut through keel bone. Push back breast halves and cut back bone in two. Next, place each body piece skin side up on cutting surface and, feeling for end of rib cage, cut each piece in half. Turn quarters skin side down and, with sharp knife or cleaver, trim skin and any visible fat from edges of each piece. Turn pieces over and prick lightly with prongs of sharp fork to help duck release its fat during cooking.

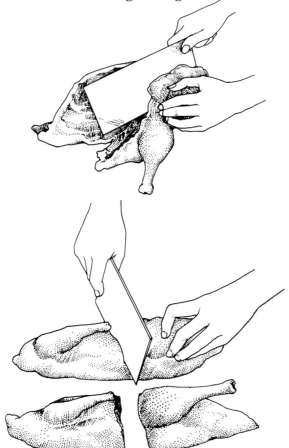

3. Place duck quarters skin side down in pot. Spoon sauce over duck, add scallions, and cover. Regulate heat so that sauce bubbles steadily at a slow boil or high simmer.

4. Cook duck 20 minutes. Turn pieces over and cook another 20 to 25 minutes.

5. When duck is done (flesh should feel slightly resilient to the touch), remove it to a chopping block and let it rest at least 5 minutes.

6. Ladle approximately 1 cup of the cooking liquid into fat separator or medium-size bowl. Let fat rise to top and discard. The degreased sauce may be put in small bowl and used as dipping sauce for duck at the table. Or, some of the sauce may be drizzled over duck before serving.

7. Remove wings and legs from duck with heavy cleaver. Chop legs crosswise at ½-inch intervals. Do same with breast pieces. Serve garnished with scallions.

Asparagus Salad

24 asparagus spears, about ½ inch in diameter
1 tablespoon dark soy sauce
2 teaspoons Oriental sesame oil
1 teaspoon Chinese rice wine vinegar
1 teaspoon sugar
1 teaspoon raw sesame seeds

1. Bring 1 quart water to a boil in covered stockpot or kettle.

2. Wash asparagus and snap off any white woody ends. Slice stalks diagonally at ½-inch intervals to form pieces about 1¼ inches long.

3. When water comes to a rolling boil, uncover pot and add asparagus. Cook 1 minute, or until just barely cooked and still crisp. Do not overcook.

4. Drain asparagus in colander under very cold running water to stop cooking as quickly as possible. Toss with 2 large wooden spoons to hasten cooling.

5. When cool, blot off any excess moisture and place in serving dish.

6. Whisk together soy sauce, sesame oil, vinegar, and sugar in small bowl until sugar is dissolved. Pour over asparagus.

7. Toast sesame seeds in small ungreased skillet over moderately high heat. Shake pan until they are golden and fragrant. Lower heat if they appear to be browning too rapidly. When they are done, remove pan from heat but keep shaking pan for a minute or two until they stop cooking from residual heat. Sprinkle sesame seeds over asparagus.

Nina Simonds

The land of rice and fish" is the local name for the fertile region along China's eastern seacoast, which includes the provinces of Chekiang, Kiangsu, Fukien, and the cosmopolitan city of Shanghai. Seafood, fresh vegetables, meat, poultry, rice, and wheat products, liberally seasoned with soy sauce and rice wine, characterize this style of cooking. Typical of the East, too, is the well-known "red-cooking" method, which involves simmering meats or poultry in a soy-based broth for a rich, flavorful stew.

Nina Simonds, cookbook author and teacher, is a particular admirer of the Shanghai style. She learned its secrets not on the mainland but on the island of Taiwan, where she apprenticed to a chef for three and a half years. Like most good cooks, however, she likes and uses Cantonese recipes, too, as well as the hot spices of the West.

Menu 1, parchment-wrapped fish and mushrooms cooked in wine, is a delicately flavored eastern-style meal. Menu 2 is a contrast: spicy spareribs, a noodle salad, and stir-fried cucumbers, all from Szechwan and Hunan. Menu 3 pairs marinated chicken shreds wrapped in lettuce leaves with another southern dish—barbecued chicken livers and water chestnuts.

When you serve the fish wrapped in paper, bring each package to the table unopened. When guests unwrap their portions, they will appreciate the burst of fragrant aroma. Serve the whole mushrooms on a nest of quickly stir-fried lettuce.

Drunken Mushrooms
Baked Fish Packages with Ham and Mushrooms
Stir-Fried Lettuce / Rice

This eastern-style meal offers an adaptation of a Chinese favorite—food cooked in a paper wrapping. Meats or fish folded in parchment or rice paper cook quickly while basting in their own juices. To finish preparing the fish and its accompaniments in this recipe, wrap all in a small square of kitchen parchment, which you can buy in hardware stores or, occasionally, in supermarkets. You may also use clean brown wrapping paper lightly oiled or aluminum foil.

To serve, loosen the paper or foil but do not remove it. You and your guests can pick out each bite with a fork or chopsticks. To cut the time you spend in the kitchen after your guests arrive, wrap the packets several hours in advance of dinner time and refrigerate them. Be sure to bring them to room temperature before baking.

In this particular recipe, the cured ham slivers add zest to the bland fish. In China, Chinese *jinhua* ham, which has a deep scarlet color and a pungent smoky taste, is traditionally used. However, Smithfield ham or prosciutto is more easily available here and is very good in this recipe. Black mushrooms have a woodlike flavor that blends well with rice wine, ginger, and scallions. Rice wine is a staple on Chinese shelves, and cooks use it in many sauces for a last-minute dash of flavor. Nina Simonds prefers using scotch as a substitute for rice wine instead of the more familiar dry sherry.

As the name implies, "drunken" dishes always feature a generous amount of wine with seafood, chicken, or other meats or, in this menu, mushrooms. Here the button mushrooms steep in the wine-enriched chicken stock and absorb the flavors of the garlic, scallions, and ginger. Because the flavor of the wine is so prominent in this recipe, use a good-quality rice wine such as *shaosing*. Otherwise, substitute a half portion of scotch.

Both recipes call for fresh ginger, an indispensable ingredient in all Chinese cooking. Ground or candied ginger is no substitute for fresh, but fortunately fresh ginger is available in most well-stocked supermarkets and at greengrocers. As the pantry section directs, always select a firm, pale brown root. If the ginger you buy is wrinkled or soft, it will not have its sharp clean taste, and you will need to use more ginger in your recipe. If your ginger is properly fresh, you do not need to peel it for mincing or chopping. For short-term storage, keep it in a cool, dry place. Otherwise wrap it tightly in foil or a plastic bag and refrigerate it. You may also peel it and put it in an airtight glass jar with enough rice wine or sherry to cover it.

WHAT TO DRINK

The delicate flavors of these dishes call for a good German Riesling, such as a Bernkasteler or Piesporter.

SHOPPING LIST AND STAPLES

4 fillets of sole or flounder (about ½ pound each)
2 paper thin slices Smithfield ham or prosciutto (about 1 to 1½ ounces)
1 pound fresh mushrooms
2 large heads Boston or leaf lettuce
1 bunch scallions
1 lemon
4 Chinese dried black mushrooms
Fresh ginger
4 cloves garlic
1¾ cups Chinese Chicken Stock (see page 13), or 2¼ cups if using scotch
2 tablespoons peanut, safflower, or corn oil
1½ teaspoons Oriental sesame oil
1 tablespoon thin soy sauce
1 cup uncooked rice
1½ teaspoons cornstarch
1 teaspoon sugar
Salt
1 cup plus 4 tablespoons Chinese rice wine or dry sherry, or ¾ cup scotch

UTENSILS

Wok
    or 12-inch skillet (for fish; lettuce)
2 medium-size saucepans, 1 with cover (for rice)
9 by 12-inch heavy baking sheet
Oval platter with sloping sides
3 small bowls
Metal colander
Measuring cups and spoons
Chinese cleaver or chef's knife
Paring knife
Metal wok spatula
2 wooden spoons
Salad spinner
4 pieces 12-inch-square kitchen parchment or aluminum foil

1. Follow general rice recipe on page 12, steps 1 and 2.
2. Follow baked fish recipe steps 1 and 2.
3. Follow stir-fried lettuce recipe steps 1 and 2, and drunken mushrooms steps 1 and 2.
4. Follow baked fish recipe steps 3 through 8.
5. Follow drunken mushrooms recipe step 3.
6. Wipe out pan and follow stir-fried lettuce recipe step 3.
7. Follow drunken mushrooms recipe step 4 and general rice recipe step 3.
8. Complete stir-fried lettuce recipe step 4, baked fish recipe step 9, rice recipe step 4, and drunken mushrooms recipe step 5. Serve.

RECIPES

Drunken Mushrooms

1 cup good quality Chinese rice wine or ½ cup scotch
1½ cups Chinese Chicken Stock, or 2 cups if using scotch
1 teaspoon salt
4 cloves garlic
4 scallions
6 quarter-size slices fresh ginger
1 pound fresh mushrooms
Juice of ½ lemon

1. Using flat side of cleaver or chef's knife, lightly crush garlic cloves, scallions, and fresh ginger.
2. Place all ingredients except mushrooms and lemon juice in heavy saucepan and bring to a boil. Boil mixture vigorously about 5 minutes.
3. Lightly rinse mushrooms and drain thoroughly. Trim stem ends and cut large caps in half. Toss in medium-size bowl with lemon juice.
4. Add mushrooms to stock and cook about 2 minutes. Turn off heat and let sit until ready to serve. Can be served warm or at room temperature.
5. To serve at table, spoon mushrooms into center of the beds of stir-fried lettuce. Sprinkle some of the broth on top.

Baked Fish Packages with Ham and Mushrooms

4 Chinese dried black mushrooms
4 fillets of sole or flounder (about ½ pound each)
The marinade:
2 quarter-size slices fresh ginger crushed with flat side of cleaver
1 teaspoon salt
1 tablespoon Chinese rice wine or scotch
The sauce:
1 tablespoon thin soy sauce
2 tablespoons Chinese rice wine or scotch
1 teaspoon sugar
½ teaspoon salt

1 teaspoon sesame oil
1½ teaspoons cornstarch
¼ cup Chinese Chicken Stock

1 tablespoon peanut, safflower, or corn oil
1 tablespoon minced scallions
2 teaspoons minced fresh ginger
2 paper-thin slices Smithfield ham or prosciutto (about 1 to 1½ ounces), cut in half crosswise to make 4 pieces

1. In small bowl, cover mushrooms with boiling water and allow to soften 20 minutes.
2. Lightly rinse fillets and pat dry. Place on oval platter and cover with marinade ingredients until ready to cook.
3. Preheat oven to 450 degrees.
4. Combine sauce ingredients in bowl.
5. Remove mushrooms from water and squeeze out excess moisture. Remove and discard stems. Cut caps into matchstick-size shreds or into long strips.
6. Heat wok or heavy skillet, add cooking oil, and heat until very hot. Add minced scallions and ginger, and stir fry about 10 seconds over high heat until fragrant. Add sauce and cook, stirring constantly, until thickened. Pour sauce back into bowl.
7. Lightly grease the squares of paper and fold in half diagonally. Open up and place 1 fish fillet on each square along the fold. Tuck ends of fillets under so that they are not too close to edge of paper. Arrange 1 piece of ham in center of each fillet. Sprinkle some of shredded mushroom on top and spoon one quarter of the sauce over all. Fold over each square to enclose the fillet and fold in edges of paper, pinching and tucking to make pleats. Repeat for remaining 3 packages.
8. Arrange packages, pleated edges up, on baking sheet. Bake packages 6 to 10 minutes, depending on thickness of fillets, or until fish flakes when prodded with a fork. (Packages will be puffed up.)
9. Place 1 package on each plate and let each person cut open his package.

Stir-Fried Lettuce

2 large heads Boston or leaf lettuce
¾ teaspoon salt
1 tablespoon Chinese rice wine or scotch
½ teaspoon sesame oil
1 tablespoon peanut, safflower, or corn oil

1. Lightly rinse lettuce in cold water and spin dry. Remove tough stems. Cut leaves into sections about 2 inches square.
2. Combine salt, wine, and sesame oil in bowl.
3. Heat wok or heavy skillet until very hot. Add cooking oil and heat until smoking. Add lettuce and sauce, and stir fry, tossing constantly, over high heat 1 minute, or until lettuce is slightly wilted. Remove pan from heat.
4. Arrange equal portions of lettuce on one side of each dinner plate, making a slight depression in center for the mushrooms.

Spicy Braised Spareribs
Tossed Noodle Salad
Stir-Fried Cucumbers with Peanut Sauce

Set out the spareribs and cucumbers on a dinner plate and on a separate dish, carefully arrange the salad on a bed of noodles.

To make the spicy spareribs in this menu, first deep fry them until they are golden brown and then braise, that is, slow-cook, them in a rich, spicy liquid. The braising liquid gradually reduces to a glaze, which coats and flavors the meat. Although the idea of braising meats is characteristic of Shanghai cooking—though not exclusive to the area—the spicing in this recipe (chili paste, scallions, and garlic) is Szechwan/Hunanese.

The Chinese do not eat Western-style salads with raw greens, but they do enjoy side dishes of cold dressed vegetables served alone or tossed with cooked noodles, as they are here.

Stir frying cucumbers may come as a new idea to American cooks. To preserve the crispness and the decorative look, be sure to cook them very quickly over a high flame. The basis for the sauce is peanut butter, as familiar in Szechwan kitchens as in American ones.

WHAT TO DRINK

This substantial menu needs a fuller-bodied, spicy wine like a Gewürztraminer. First choice here would be one from Alsace, but a California Gewürztraminer would also do very well.

52

3 pounds country-style spareribs
2 large cucumbers, preferably seedless (about 2 pounds)
½ pound fresh mung bean sprouts
3 medium-size carrots
2 medium-size zucchini
1 large bunch scallions
Fresh ginger
2 cloves garlic
2 tablespoons smooth peanut butter
2 cups plus 3 tablespoons Chinese Chicken Stock (see page 13)
1 cup plus 3 tablespoons peanut, safflower, or corn oil
4 tablespoons plus 1 teaspoon Oriental sesame oil
⅓ cup plus 6½ tablespoons thin soy sauce
2 tablespoons Chinese rice vinegar
1½ teaspoons Chinese black vinegar
3½ teaspoons chili paste
½ pound thin egg noodles, such as spaghettini or vermicelli
3 tablespoons plus 6 teaspoons sugar
1 dried hot red pepper
¼ pound roasted peanuts (optional)
¼ cup plus 4 tablespoons Chinese rice wine or scotch

UTENSILS

Stock pot
Wok
   or heavy skillet (for cucumbers)
   and small saucepan (for sauce; noodle salad)
Dutch oven with cover
2 large bowls
2 small bowls
Metal colander
Measuring cups and spoons
Chinese cleaver or chef's knife
Paring knife
Chinese mesh spoon
   or long-handled slotted metal spoon
Metal wok spatula
   or 2 long-handled wooden spoons
Vegetable peeler
Deep-fat thermometer
Rubber gloves

START-TO-FINISH STEPS

In the morning: Lightly crush ginger, scallions, and garlic, and follow braised spareribs recipe step 1.
1. Follow braised spareribs recipe steps 2 through 5.
2. While spareribs are cooking, prepare vegetables for noodle salad: rinse and drain sprouts, peel and shred carrots and zucchini, mince scallions.
3. Follow noodle salad recipe steps 1 and 2.
4. Mince scallions and ginger for stir-fried cucumber recipe, then follow steps 1 and 2.
5. Follow noodle salad recipe steps 3 and 4.
6. Complete cucumber recipe step 4.
7. Wipe out pan. Follow noodle salad recipe step 5, braised spareribs recipe step 6, and serve.

RECIPES

Spicy Braised Spareribs

3 pounds country-style spareribs

The marinade:
1½ tablespoons thin soy sauce
1 tablespoon Chinese rice wine or scotch
2 slices fresh ginger
2 scallions
2 cloves garlic

The braising mixture:
¼ cup Chinese rice wine or scotch
3 tablespoons thin soy sauce
3 tablespoons sugar
1½ cups Chinese Chicken Stock

1 cup peanut, safflower, or corn oil
2 teaspoons chili paste
1 teaspoon sesame oil

1. Have butcher cut spareribs crosswise into thirds to measure about 2½ inches in length. Trim any excessive fat and place ribs in large bowl. Combine with marinade ingredients. Seal and refrigerate until ready to cook.
2. Combine braising mixture in small bowl.
3. Heat Dutch oven and add cooking oil. Heat oil to 400 degrees on deep-fat thermometer and carefully place as many ribs in pan as will fit in one layer. Fry over high heat until golden brown on both sides, turning once. Remove with Chinese mesh spoon or long-handled slotted metal spoon and drain. Bring oil back to 400 degrees and fry

remaining ribs in same manner. Remove ribs. Carefully drain off hot oil.

4. Reheat pan and add chili paste. Stir fry several seconds over high heat. Add braising mixture and heat until boiling.

5. Add spareribs and return liquid to a boil. Reduce heat to medium and cook spareribs, partly covered, about 40 minutes, or until sauce is thick.

6. Add sesame oil and toss lightly before serving.

Tossed Noodle Salad

1 tablespoon peanut, safflower, or corn oil
½ pound thin egg noodles
1½ tablespoons sesame oil
2 cups fresh mung bean sprouts (about ½ pound), rinsed and drained
3 medium-size carrots, peeled and finely shredded (about 1 cup)
2 medium-size zucchini, finely shredded (about 1 cup)
2 tablespoons minced scallion
1 dried hot red pepper
⅓ cup thin soy sauce
3 tablespoons Chinese rice wine
4 teaspoons sugar
2 tablespoons Chinese rice vinegar
1 tablespoon sesame oil
½ cup Chinese Chicken Stock or water

1. Bring 2 quarts water and cooking oil to a boil in stockpot. Add noodles and cook until just tender.

2. Drain in colander and rinse under cold water. Drain again, place in large deep bowl, and toss with sesame oil.

3. Wearing rubber gloves, carefully halve the hot pepper and remove seeds and membrane. Mince pepper and set aside.

4. Turn noodles out onto serving platter. Arrange bean sprouts, carrots, zucchini, and scallions in circles over the noodles.

5. Place pepper and remaining ingredients in wok or small saucepan and heat until boiling. Cook about 30 seconds to allow flavors to blend. Pour over noodles before serving.

Stir-Fried Cucumbers with Peanut Sauce

2 tablespoons smooth peanut butter
2 teaspoons thin soy sauce
2 teaspoons sugar

1½ tablespoons sesame oil
1½ teaspoons Chinese black vinegar
3 tablespoons Chinese Chicken Stock
2 large cucumbers, preferably seedless (about 2 pounds)
2 tablespoons peanut, safflower, or corn oil
1 tablespoon minced scallions
2 teaspoons minced fresh ginger
1½ teaspoons chili paste
½ cup roasted peanuts for garnish (optional)

1. Combine first 6 ingredients in small bowl.

2. Peel cucumbers and cut in half lengthwise. Scoop out seeds, if necessary, and cut each half lengthwise into quarters. Roll-cut quarters (see page 10) into 1½-inch pieces.

3. Heat wok or skillet and add cooking oil. Heat until very hot. Add scallions and ginger, and stir fry about 10 seconds, until fragrant. Add chili paste and stir fry 5 seconds.

4. Add cucumbers and toss over high heat 1½ minutes. Add peanut sauce from step 1 and toss 15 seconds before serving. If desired, stir fry peanuts 10 seconds and use as garnish.

━━━━━━━━━━

ADDED TOUCH

Walnut Dust with Mandarin Orange Sections

2 eleven-ounce cans Mandarin orange sections in light syrup
¼ cup Grand Marnier
1 cup walnuts
¼ cup sugar
1½ teaspoons vanilla extract
1½ cups whipping or heavy cream

1. Drain Mandarin orange sections, reserving syrup. Combine orange sections and Grand Marnier in large mixing bowl and let soak (macerate) about 15 minutes.

2. In saucepan, bring walnuts and syrup to a boil. Skim any impurities from surface and lower heat to medium. Cook about 10 minutes until sauce has reduced to a syrupy glaze. Cool briefly and puree in blender or food processor.

3. Place sugar, vanilla extract, and cream in a chilled bowl. Using electric beater or hand mixer, beat vigorously until stiff. Fold in the pureed walnuts and orange sections. Spoon mixture into serving bowls and serve, or chill just before serving.

Barbecued Chicken Livers
Shredded Chicken in Lettuce Packages
Rice

Shredded chicken and fried rice noodles nested in lettuce leaves are served with skewered chicken livers and vegetables.

The emphasis of Cantonese cooking is always on enhancing the flavor of the main ingredients, not overpowering it. Therefore, Cantonese chefs use chopped fresh ginger, minced garlic, and soy sauce—their basic flavoring agents—with care and restraint. The result is a much milder kind of cooking than the heartier, spicier Szechwan style. Cantonese cooking also tends to be less oily than any of the other regional styles. This chicken liver recipe is a good example of southern Chinese cooking because the barbecue sauce is mild, and its ingredients complement the taste of the liver.

The second dish is marinated, shredded chicken strips deliciously combined with pine nuts, water chestnuts, and dried Chinese mushrooms and served over fried rice noodles nested in crisp lettuce leaves. Invite your guests to

roll the leaves around the filling to make a Chinese-style sandwich.

The dried rice noodles, also known as *maifun*, that accompany the chicken add a delicious crunch to the "sandwich." The noodles expand when deep fried to become very light and crisp. Made from rice flour, they are popular in southern China, one of the nation's major rice-growing regions.

WHAT TO DRINK

A dry to slightly off-dry white wine will complement this meal. A California Sauvignon Blanc, a French Vouvray, or an Italian Pinot Grigio would all do nicely. More unusual but also very good would be a New York Seyval Blanc.

1 pound skinless, boneless chicken breasts (about 2 whole breasts)

12 whole chicken livers (about 1 pound)

1 head iceberg lettuce

1 large bunch scallions

3 cloves garlic

5 Chinese dried black mushrooms

Fresh ginger

3 eight-ounce cans water chestnuts

¼ cup *hoisin* sauce

2 tablespoons duck or plum sauce

4 cups peanut, corn, or safflower oil

3½ teaspoons Oriental sesame oil

6 tablespoons thin soy sauce

8-ounce package thin Chinese rice noodles (*maifun*) or cellophane noodles

1 cup uncooked rice

1½ tablespoons plus 2 teaspoons sugar

3 teaspoons cornstarch

Salt

2 ounces pine nuts

5 tablespoons Chinese rice wine or scotch

UTENSILS

Dutch oven

Heavy 12-inch skillet

Large saucepan

Medium-size saucepan with cover (for rice)

Heatproof broiling pan

9 by 12-inch baking sheet

Large bowl

Medium-size bowl

2 small bowls

Metal colander

Measuring cups and spoons

Chinese cleaver or chef's knife

Paring knife

Chinese mesh spoon or long-handled slotted metal spoon

Metal wok spatula or 2 wooden spoons

Deep-fat thermometer

8 bamboo skewers

START-TO-FINISH STEPS

1. Follow shredded chicken recipe steps 1 through 3.

2. Follow chicken livers recipe steps 1 through 4.

3. Follow general rice recipe on page 12, steps 1 and 2.

4. Follow shredded chicken recipe steps 4 through 7.

5. Follow general rice recipe step 3.

6. Follow shredded chicken recipe step 8.

7. Follow chicken livers recipe steps 5 through 7.

8. While chicken livers are broiling, complete shredded chicken recipe steps 9 through 11 and general rice recipe step 4. Serve chicken livers, step 8, at once.

RECIPES

Barbecued Chicken Livers

12 canned water chestnuts, drained and halved

12 whole chicken livers (about 1 pound), trimmed of fat

4 to 5 scallions, cut into 1-inch lengths or longer

¼ cup *hoisin* sauce

2 tablespoons duck or plum sauce

2 tablespoons thin soy sauce

2 tablespoons Chinese rice wine or scotch

1½ tablespoons sugar

1 teaspoon sesame oil

3 cloves garlic, crushed

1. Bring 1 quart water to a boil in large saucepan and blanch water chestnuts 30 seconds. With Chinese mesh or long-handled slotted metal spoon, remove from water and drain in colander. Soak bamboo skewers in warm water.

2. Cut chicken livers in 3 or 4 pieces and blanch 1 minute. Drain in colander and rinse under cold running water.

3. Pat dry and place in large bowl along with the water chestnuts.

4. Add remaining ingredients to water chestnuts and livers. Toss well. Marinate 20 minutes or until ready to cook.

5. Preheat broiler.

6. On each of 8 bamboo skewers, thread a scallion piece crosswise, then a water chestnut and a chicken liver. Repeat two more times, ending with a scallion piece, so that each skewer is threaded with 4 scallion sections, 3 water chestnuts, and 3 chicken livers each. Arrange skewers in heatproof pan and spoon marinade on top.

7. Place pan about 3 inches from heat source and broil 5 to 7 minutes, turning once, until livers are golden but still pink in center.

8. Serve immediately.

Shredded Chicken in Lettuce Packages

5 Chinese dried black mushrooms
2 cups canned water chestnuts, drained
1 pound skinless, boneless chicken breasts (about 2 whole breasts)

The marinade:
1 tablespoon thin soy sauce
1 tablespoon Chinese rice wine or scotch
1 teaspoon sesame oil
2 tablespoons water
1½ teaspoons cornstarch

The sauce:
3 tablespoons thin soy sauce
2 tablespoons Chinese rice wine or scotch
2 teaspoons sugar
1½ teaspoons salt
1½ teaspoons sesame oil
½ cup Chinese Chicken Stock or water
1½ teaspoons cornstarch

16 lettuce leaves, rinsed and drained
4 cups peanut, corn, or safflower oil
1 ounce thin Chinese rice noodles (*maifun*) or cellophane noodles
¼ cup pine nuts
1 tablespoon minced scallions
1 tablespoon minced fresh ginger

1. In small bowl, cover mushrooms with hot water and allow to soften, about 15 minutes, or until spongy. Bring 2 cups water to a boil in large saucepan and blanch water chestnuts 30 seconds. Drain and slice. Set aside.
2. Cut breasts in half lengthwise and then once again in half crosswise. Cut lengthwise again into matchstick-size shreds, about 2 inches long and ⅛ inch thick.
3. Combine marinade ingredients with chicken strips in medium-size bowl, and toss to coat. Marinate 15 minutes.
4. Drain mushrooms, cut off stems, and shred caps. Stir to combine sauce ingredients in small bowl.
5. Arrange lettuce on platter and refrigerate.
6. Preheat oven to 325 degrees. Toast pine nuts on baking sheet 3 to 5 minutes, shaking pan from time to time. Remove from oven.
7. In Dutch oven, add cooking oil and heat to 400 degrees on deep-fat thermometer or until smoking. Drop rice noodles into oil and deep fry several seconds until puffed and lightly golden. Turn over and deep fry a few more seconds.

Remove with Chinese mesh spoon or long-handled slotted metal spoon to drain on paper towels and cool. Turn heat to low. Transfer to serving platter and with your fingers break up noodles to form a bed for chicken mixture.
8. Add chicken shreds. Stir constantly to separate the shreds and cook until they turn white. Remove with slotted metal spoon and drain on paper towels.
9. Heat large heavy skillet and add 3 tablespoons of the hot cooking oil from the Dutch oven. Add scallions and ginger, and stir fry with wok spatula or 2 wooden spoons 10 seconds until fragrant. Add shredded mushrooms and stir fry another 10 seconds. Then add water chestnuts and toss lightly over high heat about 20 seconds.
10. Add sauce and stir until thickened. Add chicken shreds and pine nuts. Toss lightly over high heat to coat. Spoon chicken over the rice noodles.
11. Remove lettuce from the refrigerator. Let each person spoon a portion of chicken-and-noodles into a lettuce leaf. To eat, roll up the leaf to enclose the filling.

ADDED TOUCH

Apples with Honey and Candied Ginger

4 firm apples, such as Delicious or Rome Beauty
1 lemon
2 tablespoons honey
4 quarter-size slices candied ginger, cut into shreds
½ to 1 teaspoon cinnamon, or to taste
4 scoops vanilla ice cream

1. Peel apples and rub surface with a cut lemon half. Cut about ½-inch-thick slice squarely off top of each apple and set aside. (This slice will serve as a lid.) Using melon baller, remove core and seeds from lid and main body of each apple. Sprinkle inside with lemon juice.
2. Arrange apples upright in heatproof 9-inch pie plate or quiche pan. (If they will not stand upright, cut thin slice off bottom of each apple.) Spoon ½ tablespoon of honey into cavity of each apple and sprinkle with ginger and cinnamon. Cover apples with their "lids."
3. Bring 1½ inches water to a boil in wok or deep skillet. Place plate in steamer tray or on trivet and set over boiling water. Cover and steam 15 to 25 minutes over high heat, or until tender. Carefully check water level from time to time, replenishing as needed.
4. Remove lids of each apple and place a scoop of ice cream in each. Replace lids and serve.

Michael Tong

M ichael Tong was born in Shanghai and spent his childhood first in Taiwan, then in Hong Kong, acquiring a love for both northern- and southern-style Chinese food. Now a New Yorker, he operates three Manhattan restaurants—an occupation that leaves him time to cook for himself and his friends only as a hobby. As a result, he favors uncomplicated recipes, easily available ingredients, and an interesting variety of cooking techniques. He believes that knowing how to use many techniques is important because each contributes to the diversity of texture and flavor of the dishes.

All of Michael Tong's menus are family style, which means the dishes are particularly quick to prepare and should be served all together. And because the recipes use simple ingredients, they appeal to everyone's taste. Quick as his menus are, Mr. Tong likes to simplify things even further by preparing his meals in stages—perhaps the appetizer and soup in the morning, then the entrée at mealtime. Whether you follow this advice or cook the meal all at once, you should be able to do it in twenty minutes if you gather and organize your ingredients carefully. A further piece of advice: mix your sauce ingredients first rather than add them to the dish separately. In this way, you can take a moment to adjust the sauce to your own taste, then add it to the dish with confidence.

Tender white scallops garnished with scallions and chopped parsley look appetizing against the reddish-brown pork cubes and the green vegetables. Easy to prepare, this meal is also quick to serve. Simply arrange your four plates as you finish cooking and carry them to the table.

Sautéed Scallops
Pork with Barbecue Sauce
Broccoli with Snow Peas / Rice

In this meal the scallops are Shanghainese and the pork in barbecue sauce is Cantonese. Though these recipes are modern adaptations, the tastes and textures are true to their traditional roots. Michael Tong believes that techniques are more crucial to any given dish than are its ingredients. For instance, if you cannot find fresh bay or sea scallops, buy a firm white-fleshed fish instead and cube it. Or, if you prefer, substitute boned chicken breasts for the pork in the second recipe: chicken works equally well, though it cooks more quickly, and gives the dish a different taste.

For best results in this menu, the snow peas, or sugar snap peas, if you prefer, should be ultrafresh—crisp and bright with the tiny peas just visible inside. To store these peas until you are ready to cook them, wrap the unwashed pods in a perforated plastic bag and refrigerate. This way they will last from four to five days. Before cooking them with the broccoli, snap off the ends and peel off the strings. If you decide to try frozen snow peas instead, cook them just long enough to get them hot. Otherwise, they will become soggy.

Broccoli, generally available fresh all year, should have a fresh green color in the leaves and head. An aging head of broccoli will have started to yellow. Broccoli stalks should be firm. To store a head of broccoli, wash it well, then wrap it in a plastic bag, and refrigerate.

When cooking the vegetables, watch them carefully. The broccoli, like the snow peas, should be crunchy and firm to the bite.

WHAT TO DRINK

According to Michael Tong, not all American or European wines go well with Chinese food. For this menu, he suggests an Alsatian white or a California Chenin Blanc.

SHOPPING LIST AND STAPLES

1 pound boneless pork, or 2 pounds thin pork chops
1 pound fresh bay or sea scallops
1 large bunch broccoli
½ pound snow peas
1 small carrot (optional)
1 bunch scallions
1 bunch coriander
Fresh ginger
3 cloves garlic

2 eggs
¼ cup Chinese Chicken Stock (see page 13)
2 tablespoons Oriental barbecue sauce, preferably, or *hoisin* sauce
7 cups plus 3 tablespoons vegetable oil
4 tablespoons plus ½ teaspoon sesame oil
2 tablespoons light soy sauce
1 cup uncooked rice
3 tablespoons plus 3½ teaspoons cornstarch
½ teaspoon sugar
Salt
¾ teaspoon white pepper
¾ cup plus 2 tablespoons plus 2 teaspoons dry sherry

UTENSILS

Wok
    or Dutch oven (for deep frying scallops; pork)
    and heavy 12-inch skillet (for stir frying scallops; pork; broccoli)
Medium-size saucepan with cover (for rice)
2 large mixing bowls
Medium-size bowl
4 small bowls
Metal colander
Measuring cups and spoons
Chinese cleaver or chef's knife
Paring knife
Metal wok spatula or 2 long-handled wooden spoons
Chinese mesh spoon or long-handled slotted metal spoon
Deep-fat thermometer

START-TO-FINISH STEPS

1. Follow general rice recipe on page 12, steps 1 and 2.
2. Follow pork recipe steps 1 through 3.
3. Preheat oven to 200 degrees. Continue pork recipe, steps 4 through 7.
4. Wipe out pan. Pare broccoli, removing stems, and cut flowerets into small pieces.
5. Follow general rice recipe step 3.
6. Follow sautéed scallops recipe steps 1 through 6 and keep warm in oven.
7. Wipe out pan and cook broccoli with snow peas, steps 1 through 4. Follow general rice recipe step 4. Serve with pork, sautéed scallops, and vegetables.

Sautéed Scallops

1 pound fresh bay or sea scallops
1 tablespoon cornstarch
3 cups vegetable oil

The sauce:
1 teaspoon salt
½ cup dry sherry
1 teaspoon cornstarch
¼ teaspoon white pepper

2 teaspoons chopped fresh ginger
3 scallions, white part cut into rings, green part into
    julienne strips
2 teaspoons chopped fresh coriander
2 tablespoons sesame oil
1 small carrot, cut into julienne pieces for garnish
    (optional)

1. If using sea scallops, cut them in half. Combine with 1 tablespoon cornstarch in large bowl and toss to coat.
2. Heat vegetable oil in wok or Dutch oven until almost smoking.
3. Combine sauce ingredients in small bowl.
4. Add scallops to pan, stirring to separate, and cook 3 to 4 minutes, or until they float to top of oil. Remove with Chinese mesh spoon or long-handled slotted metal spoon and drain in colander lined with paper towels. If using wok, carefully pour off oil into a container.
5. Heat wok or large heavy skillet and add ginger, scallion rings, and coriander. Sauté 30 seconds, then add scallops and sauce ingredients. Cook until scallops are well coated and heated through. Swirl in sesame oil.
6. Mound scallops in center of heated serving plate and garnish the edges, if you wish, with the carrots and green scallion strips.

Pork with Barbecue Sauce

1 pound boneless pork, or 2 pounds thin pork chops
2 egg whites
1 tablespoon cornstarch
2 teaspoons dry sherry
¼ teaspoon salt
¼ teaspoon white pepper

The sauce:
2 scallions, white part only, cut into julienne pieces
2 teaspoons chopped fresh ginger
2 to 3 teaspoons chopped garlic
¼ cup dry sherry
2 tablespoons light soy sauce
¼ teaspoon white pepper
2 tablespoons Oriental barbecue sauce, preferably, or
    hoisin sauce
1 teaspoon cornstarch mixed with 2 teaspoons water

4 cups vegetable oil
2 tablespoons sesame oil

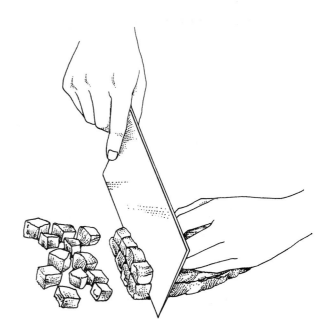

1. Cut pork into ½-inch cubes (see diagram). If using pork chops, remove meat and discard bones.
2. Lightly beat egg whites in large bowl. Add cubed pork, tossing to coat well. Stir together cornstarch, sherry, salt, and pepper in small bowl. Add to pork and with your fingers toss to combine.
3. With a fork, combine sauce ingredients in small bowl.
4. Heat vegetable oil in wok or Dutch oven until almost smoking (about 350 degrees on deep-fat thermometer).
5. Add pork cubes a few at a time to prevent sticking. Cook until golden brown, about 3 minutes. Remove with Chinese mesh spoon or long-handled slotted metal spoon to drain in metal colander. Repeat until all the meat is cooked. If using wok, pour off oil into a container.
6. Heat wok or large heavy skillet and add sauce and drained pork. Cook until thickened and blended. Swirl in sesame oil.
7. Pour pork and sauce onto heated serving plate and keep warm in preheated 200-degree oven.

Broccoli with Snow Peas

3 tablespoons vegetable oil
1 large bunch broccoli, stems removed and flowerets cut
    into small pieces
½ pound snow peas (about 30)
¼ cup Chinese Chicken Stock
2 tablespoons dry sherry
¼ teaspoon salt
½ teaspoon sugar
1 tablespoon cornstarch mixed with 1 tablespoon water
½ teaspoon sesame oil

1. In wok or large heavy skillet, heat oil until almost smoking.
2. Add broccoli and snow peas. Stir fry 30 seconds.
3. Add stock, sherry, salt, and sugar. Cook at a boil 2 minutes.
4. Add cornstarch mixture and sesame oil. Toss 30 seconds until well coated. Serve.

Egg Drop Soup with Tomato
Orange Beef
Stir-Fried Bok Choy / Rice

Every dish in this family-style meal features festive color, so you need no garnish. Serving pieces are simple, too.

This meal features egg drop soup, thick with threads of yolk that form when you stir beaten eggs into the hot chicken broth. This version includes chopped fresh tomatoes.

Bok choy, a variety of Chinese cabbage, has white fleshy stems and dark green leaves. When cooked, it is both tender and sweet. If it is not available, you may substitute such lettuces as Romaine or leaf lettuce.

WHAT TO DRINK

This is an excellent combination of flavors to show off a Moselle wine: choose a Wehlener or an Erdener.

SHOPPING LIST AND STAPLES

1 pound flank steak

1 head bok choy (about 1½ to 2 pounds)
1 large tomato
1 red bell pepper
1 small yellow squash
1 bunch scallions
Fresh ginger
4 eggs
1 quart plus ½ cup Chinese Chicken Stock
   (see page 13)
3 cups plus 3 tablespoons vegetable oil
1 tablespoon plus 1 teaspoon Oriental sesame oil
2 tablespoons light soy sauce
¼ cup white vinegar
7 tablespoons cornstarch
¼ cup plus ½ teaspoon sugar
3 tablespoons dried orange peel, or 2 tablespoons fresh
   grated orange rind
Salt

¼ teaspoon white pepper
½ cup plus 2 tablespoons plus 2 teaspoons dry sherry

UTENSILS

Wok
    or Dutch oven (for deep frying flank steak)
    and heavy 12-inch skillet (for stir frying flank steak; bok
      choy)
2 medium-size saucepans, 1 with cover (for rice)
Medium-size bowl
4 small bowls
Metal colander
Measuring cups and spoons
Chinese cleaver or chef's knife
Paring knife
Chinese mesh spoon or long-handled slotted metal spoon
16-inch chopsticks or long-handled wooden spoon

START-TO-FINISH STEPS

1. Follow orange beef recipe steps 1 through 4.
2. Prepare bok choy, step 1.
3. Preheat oven to 200 degrees. Cook orange beef, steps 5 through 10.
4. Follow egg drop soup recipe steps 1 and 2.
5. Wipe out pan. Follow bok choy recipe steps 2 and 3.
6. Follow egg drop soup recipe steps 3 through 5, bok choy recipe step 4, and serve with orange beef.

RECIPES

Egg Drop Soup with Tomato

1 large tomato
1 quart Chinese Chicken Stock
¼ teaspoon salt
2 teaspoons dry sherry
3 tablespoons cornstarch blended with 3 tablespoons
    water
2 eggs, lightly beaten
1 teaspoon sesame oil

1. Bring 1 cup water to a boil in medium-size saucepan and blanch tomato 1 minute. Remove with slotted metal spoon. Cool slightly and chop. You should have about ¾ cup.
2. Put tomato and stock in same saucepan and bring to a boil. Cook over high heat 2 minutes.
3. Stir in salt, sherry, and cornstarch mixture, and cook 1 minute.
4. Slowly add beaten eggs in a stream, stirring with chopsticks or a wooden spoon. Swirl in sesame oil.
5. Pour into soup tureen or individual bowls.

Orange Beef

1 pound flank steak
2 egg whites

3 tablespoons cornstarch
½ cup dry sherry
2 tablespoons light soy sauce
¼ cup sugar
¼ cup white vinegar
¼ teaspoon white pepper
3 cups vegetable oil
1 red bell pepper
4 scallions, white part only
1 small yellow squash
3 tablespoons dried orange peel, or 2 tablespoons fresh
    grated orange rind
1 tablespoon sesame oil

1. Using cleaver or chef's knife, slice flank steak on diagonal into ¼-inch slices. Stack slices and cut into ¼-inch strips.
2. Lightly beat egg whites in medium-size bowl and add flank steak. With your fingers mix well.
3. Sprinkle in 2 tablespoons of the cornstarch and mix well.
4. Combine remaining cornstarch and next five ingredients in small bowl, stirring to dissolve cornstarch.
5. Heat oil in wok or Dutch oven until almost smoking.
6. Core and seed pepper, and cut into diagonal chunks.
7. Cut scallions lengthwise into thin slices.
8. Cut squash into quarters, then into matchstick-size pieces.
9. When oil is almost smoking, carefully add flank steak piece by piece using Chinese mesh spoon or slotted metal spoon, stirring so that pieces do not stick together. Toss them in oil until they turn dark golden brown, about 1 minute. Add red pepper and cook 1 minute. Remove meat and pepper with the spoon and drain in colander. If using wok, carefully pour off oil into a container.
10. Heat wok or large deep skillet and add sesame oil, scallions, squash, and orange peel. Wait 30 seconds, then add meat, peppers, and sauce. Cook, tossing and stirring, until thickened. Transfer food to heated serving platter and keep warm in 200-degree oven.

Stir-Fried Bok Choy

1 head bok choy (about 1½ to 2 pounds)
2 tablespoons dry sherry
1 tablespoon cornstarch blended with 1 teaspoon water
3 tablespoons vegetable oil
½ tablespoon chopped fresh ginger
½ teaspoon salt
½ teaspoon sugar
½ cup Chinese Chicken Stock

1. Chop off tops of bok choy leaves and discard. Cut remaining leaves in half and then lengthwise into ¼-inch slices. Rinse and pat dry with paper towels.
2. Heat wok or skillet and add vegetable oil. When almost smoking, add ginger and bok choy. Stir fry 30 seconds.
3. Add stock, salt, sugar, and sherry. Cook 2 minutes.
4. Stir cornstarch mixture again and add to pan. Cook, stirring just until thickened, about 30 seconds.

Bean Curd Salad with Peanuts
Steamed Sea Bass with Black Bean Sauce
Chicken, Szechwan Style / Rice

Bean curd salad and whole steamed fish look especially attractive if you arrange them on beds of fresh green lettuce.

This meal also offers some regional contrasts: the steamed sea bass is typically Cantonese, and the bean curd salad with peanuts and the chicken are spicy Szechwan-style dishes. Cooks in the western provinces frequently use nuts to flavor their dishes, their favorites being almonds, cashews, walnuts, and peanuts. For this particular recipe, use regular unsalted peanuts if the dried variety are not available. The salad is excellent for other meals as well, particularly picnics.

WHAT TO DRINK

An Italian Pinot Grigio or Verdicchio or a French Muscadet will all provide dryness, fruit, and acidity to complement the meal.

SHOPPING LIST AND STAPLES

1 whole skinless, boneless chicken breast (about 1 pound)
2-pound fresh whole sea bass, boned and butterflied, or 1½ pounds fillets
4 large squares fresh firm bean curd
1 tablespoon Chinese fermented black beans
1 red bell pepper
1 small head curly lettuce (optional)
2 bunches scallions
1 bunch coriander
Fresh ginger
1 clove garlic
2 eggs
3 cups plus 1 tablespoon vegetable oil
2 tablespoons plus 2 teaspoons sesame oil
1 teaspoon sesame chili oil (optional)
3 tablespoons light soy sauce
¼ pound dry roasted peanuts (optional)
1 cup uncooked rice
2 tablespoons plus 1 teaspoon cornstarch
1½ teaspoons sugar
Salt
White pepper
¼ cup plus 3 tablespoons dry sherry

UTENSILS

Stockpot or 12-inch sauté pan with cover
Wok or Dutch oven (for chicken)
Medium-size saucepan with cover (for rice)
2 large mixing bowls

Medium-size bowl
3 small bowls
Oval plate with sloping sides for steaming fish
Metal colander
Metal trivet
Measuring cups and spoons
Chinese cleaver or chef's knife
Paring knife
Metal wok spatula or long-handled wooden spoon
Chinese mesh spoon or long-handled slotted metal spoon

START-TO-FINISH STEPS

1. For steamed sea bass recipe, slice and cut ginger into thin strips and cut white part of scallions into thin strips.
2. Prepare steamed sea bass, steps 1 through 3.
3. While fish is steaming, follow general rice recipe on page 12, steps 1 and 2.
4. Chop scallions and coriander for bean curd salad, and ginger, scallions, garlic, and red bell pepper for Szechwan chicken.
5. Follow Szechwan chicken recipe steps 1 through 7.
6. Follow general rice recipe step 3.
7. Make bean curd salad, steps 1 through 3.
8. Follow general rice recipe step 4, Szechwan chicken recipe step 8, and steamed sea bass step 4. Serve.

RECIPES

Bean Curd Salad with Peanuts

4 large squares fresh firm bean curd
1 teaspoon chopped fresh ginger
2 tablespoons chopped scallion, white part only
1½ teaspoons chopped fresh coriander
1 teaspoon sesame chili oil (optional)
1 tablespoon dry sherry
1 tablespoon light soy sauce
2 teaspoons sesame oil
½ teaspoon salt
½ teaspoon sugar
3 tablespoons dry roasted peanuts for garnish (optional)

1. Cut bean curd squares into ¼-inch cubes and place in medium-size bowl.
2. Sprinkle remaining ingredients except peanuts over bean curd and with your fingers toss lightly to blend.
3. Mound salad on serving plate with lettuce and tomato, and sprinkle with peanuts for garnish, if desired.

Steamed Sea Bass with Black Bean Sauce

2-pound fresh whole sea bass, boned and butterflied, or
    1½ pounds fillets
7 quarter-size thin slices fresh ginger, cut into thin strips
4 scallions, white part only, cut into thin strips
1 tablespoon Chinese fermented black beans
½ teaspoon salt
2 tablespoons dry sherry

1 teaspoon white pepper
1 tablespoon vegetable oil
Curly lettuce for garnish (optional)

1. Bring ½ inch water to a boil in stockpot or large sauté pan.
2. Make a diagonal slit on both sides of whole fish or in each fish fillet and wash fish under cold running water to remove any debris and blood. Place fish cut side up on an oval plate slightly smaller than steaming vessel.
3. Combine remaining ingredients in small bowl and sprinkle over fish. Set plate on metal trivet in pan. Cover tightly and steam fish 20 minutes, or until fish flakes easily and is opaque. Check water level occasionally.
4. To serve, place plate in which fish was steamed directly onto another larger platter. Garnish with lettuce, if desired.

Chicken, Szechwan Style

1 whole skinless, boneless chicken breast (about 1 pound)
2 egg whites
2 tablespoons cornstarch plus 1 teaspoon cornstarch
    mixed with 2 teaspoons water

The sauce:
½ teaspoon white pepper
2 tablespoons light soy sauce
¼ cup dry sherry
1 teaspoon sugar
2 tablespoons sesame oil

3 cups vegetable oil
2 teaspoons chopped fresh ginger
2 scallions, white part only, sliced into thin rings
1 teaspoon chopped garlic
1 red bell pepper, cut into ¼-inch strips and then into
    diagonal pieces

1. Hold cleaver or chef's knife parallel to work surface and cut chicken breast in half, making thin pieces. Cut each piece into 1-inch dice.
2. Lightly beat egg whites in large bowl. Add chicken and mix well. Add 2 tablespoons cornstarch and mix well so that chicken pieces are evenly coated.
3. Combine sauce ingredients plus cornstarch mixture in small bowl.
4. Heat oil in wok or Dutch oven over medium-high heat until almost smoking.
5. Place ginger, scallions, and garlic in small bowl.
6. When oil is almost smoking, gently add chicken pieces, a few at a time, and stir so that they do not stick together. Toss chicken in the oil about 2 minutes. Add red pepper and stir with metal wok spatula 30 seconds.
7. Carefully pour chicken and peppers into metal colander set over large bowl to catch the oil.
8. Reheat pan and add ginger, garlic, and scallions. Wait 1 second, then add chicken and sauce ingredients. Toss to coat chicken and combine flavors. Remove to heated serving platter.

Jeri Sipe

MENU 1 (Right)
Sweet and Sour Cucumber Salad
Quick Barbecued Pork
Fish Steaks with Hot Sauce
Rice

MENU 2
Pink Chinese Radishes
Spicy Fried Calf's Liver
Mountain Snow White Chicken
Rice

MENU 3
Vegetable Balls with Sweet and Sour Sauce
Spicy Lamb with Tree Ear Mushrooms
Sautéed Shrimp with Cucumbers
Rice

The thrifty Chinese waste nothing edible. Ingenious and practical, they have recipes for even the most humble ingredients. Their skilled cooks can extend small portions of food to feed many and still retain peak flavor and aroma. Jeri Sipe, an Oregon-based cooking teacher who was born and raised in Taiwan, shows her students how to practice this kitchen economy. She stresses the use of fresh ingredients, never overcooked, but believes that cooks can concoct a fine Chinese meal with leftovers if the food was fresh and of high quality to begin with.

Before coming to the United States, Jeri Sipe cooked professionally in Taiwan for many years, learning traditional recipes and techniques. She interprets them in these three menus, all of which have their roots in northern Chinese and Taiwanese styles—that is, they are imaginative blendings of both the sweet and the spicy. Menus 1 and 3 particularly demonstrate this blending: tangy meats are contrasted with the cool, sweet taste of vegetables. Like any accomplished Chinese cook, Jeri Sipe strives to balance tastes and to avoid serving a meal that completely overwhelms the palate. Menu 3 features a typical Taiwanese specialty—vegetable balls. Served with a sweet and sour sauce, they make a delicious appetizer.

To set the table for this meal, you need serving platters for the main courses and small side dishes to hold the toasted sesame seeds, hot pepper sauce, and mustard sauce. Pass the sauces, or provide a bowl of each sauce for each guest. To unify your setting, use color-coordinated dishes that have contrasting shapes.

Sweet and Sour Cucumber Salad
Quick Barbecued Pork
Fish Steaks with Hot Sauce / Rice

This recipe calls for pork shoulder, an economical cut, which you slice for barbecuing. If you wish, substitute a leaner cut—boneless loin, for example. It will cost more per pound but will be considerably lower in fat, and you will have fewer scraps to throw away.

One of the subtle tastes in the marinade for the pork is Chinese five-spice, which Chinese cooks use in every form of regional cuisine. It should be part of your regular Chinese pantry, and you can blend it at home if you like. Simply combine roughly equal portions of cinnamon stick, cloves, brown Szechwan peppercorns, fennel, and star anise in a blender, and grind them fine.

Serve the pork with two simple dipping sauces, as directed in the recipe. The first — catsup, hot pepper sauce, and Worcestershire—can be as mild or as hot as you like, depending on the amount of hot pepper sauce you add, and the mustard sauce is very hot. The toasted sesame seeds provide another flavorful, crunchy dip for the pork.

Fresh swordfish, if you can find it, is a dry, white, meaty fish and the best choice for this recipe. If you cannot get it or prefer something less expensive, halibut or any other thick, boneless fish steak will also work well. Be sure to rinse the fish steaks and pat them dry with paper towels before beginning the recipe.

The piquant sauce served with the fish provides another spicy yet contrasting flavor. The recipe calls for two fresh or dried hot red chili peppers. If you cannot find the Chinese variety, look for other Asian varieties, usually found in Oriental shops. Otherwise, use the regular crushed red chili peppers sold in jars at most supermarkets, although they are not as strong or as flavorful. One teaspoon is equal to one small dried red chili.

The sweet and sour cucumber is the cooling taste contrast for the whole meal. Start with cold cucumbers and then return them to the refrigerator after you have set them to marinate.

WHAT TO DRINK

The variety of flavors here will fight most wines, so opt for cold beer, ale, or tea.

SHOPPING LIST AND STAPLES

1 pound pork shoulder
2 swordfish or halibut steaks (about 10 ounces each),
   1 inch thick

2 cucumbers
1 bunch scallions
2 fresh or dried hot red peppers
Fresh ginger
½ cup beef or Chinese Chicken Stock (see page 13)
1 tablespoon *hoisin* sauce
2 teaspoons oyster sauce
3 tablespoons catsup
4¼ cups peanut or vegetable oil
1½ teaspoons sesame oil
1 tablespoon light soy sauce plus 1 tablespoon (optional)
1 tablespoon mushroom soy sauce (optional)
Hot pepper sauce
Worcestershire sauce
3 teaspoons white distilled vinegar
1 teaspoon chili paste
2 teaspoons honey
1 cup uncooked rice
1½ tablespoons potato starch, preferably, or cornstarch
1¼ teaspoons cornstarch
3 tablespoons sugar
1 teaspoon brown sugar
Pinch Chinese five-spice
1 tablespoon hot mustard powder
Salt
2 tablespoons toasted sesame seeds
3½ tablespoons ginger wine or dry sherry

UTENSILS

Wok
   or Dutch oven (for pork)
   and 12-inch skillet (for fish)
Medium-size saucepan with cover (for rice)
Small saucepan
Baking pan
Medium-size bowl
2 small bowls
3 small serving bowls
Metal colander
Measuring cups and spoons
Chinese cleaver or chef's knife
Paring knife
Metal wok spatula or Western spatula
Chinese mesh spoon or long-handled slotted metal spoon
Deep-fat thermometer
Vegetable peeler

1. Follow general rice recipe on page 12, steps 1 and 2.
2. Follow sweet and sour cucumber recipe step 1.
3. Follow barbecued pork recipe steps 1 and 2.
4. Follow fish steaks recipe steps 1 through 5.
5. Follow sweet and sour cucumber recipe step 2.
6. Preheat oven to 200 degrees and complete barbecued pork recipe, steps 3 through 7.
7. Follow general rice recipe step 3.
8. Follow sweet and sour cucumber recipe step 3.
9. Wipe out pan and cook fish steaks, steps 6 through 11. Follow barbecued pork recipe step 8, rice recipe step 4, and bring everything to the table.

RECIPES

Sweet and Sour Cucumber Salad

2 cucumbers
1 teaspoon salt
3 teaspoons vinegar
3 tablespoons sugar

1. Peel cucumbers and slice in half lengthwise. Scoop out seeds and slice halves crosswise into ⅛-inch pieces. Place them in colander and mix well with salt. Let stand 15 minutes.
2. Drain off salty water. Put cucumbers in small bowl and add vinegar and sugar. Let stand 10 minutes.
3. Before serving, squeeze and drain sweet and sour juice from cucumber slices. Place cucumbers in serving bowl.

Quick Barbecued Pork

1 pound pork shoulder
The marinade:
1 tablespoon *hoisin* sauce
Pinch Chinese five-spice
1 tablespoon light soy sauce
1½ tablespoons ginger wine or dry sherry
2 teaspoons honey
½ teaspoon sesame oil
1½ tablespoons potato starch, preferably, or cornstarch

3 tablespoons catsup
4 drops hot pepper sauce
¼ teaspoon Worcestershire sauce
1 tablespoon hot mustard powder
2 tablespoons warm water
2 tablespoons toasted sesame seeds
4 cups peanut or vegetable oil

1. Slice pork horizontally into ½-inch slices, then cut into strips about 3 inches long and ½ inch wide.
2. Combine marinade ingredients in medium-size bowl and add pork. Mix thoroughly and let stand 10 minutes or longer.
3. Mix catsup, hot pepper sauce, and Worcestershire in small serving bowl.

4. In another small bowl, stir mustard powder and water until a thick paste is formed. Cover with plastic wrap.
5. Put sesame seeds in third small serving bowl.
6. Heat cooking oil in wok or Dutch oven to 375 degrees on deep-fat thermometer. Carefully add pork and any of the marinade left in bowl, and cook about 2 minutes. Use metal wok spatula or slotted metal spoon to stir pork and keep it from sticking together.
7. Remove pork from oil with Chinese mesh spoon or long-handled slotted metal spoon and drain well. Place on serving platter and keep warm in oven.
8. When ready to serve, garnish with some sesame seeds, if desired, and serve with the hot sauce, mustard, and sesame seeds as dips.

Fish Steaks with Hot Sauce

2 swordfish or halibut steaks (about 10 ounces each),
    1 inch thick
½ cup beef or Chinese Chicken Stock
2 teaspoons oyster sauce
1¼ teaspoons cornstarch
1 teaspoon chili paste
1 teaspoon sesame oil
4 scallions
3 slices fresh ginger
2 fresh or dried hot red peppers
¼ cup peanut or vegetable oil
1 teaspoon brown sugar
1 tablespoon mushroom soy sauce or light soy sauce
2 tablespoons ginger wine or dry sherry

1. Rinse fish under cold running water and pat dry.
2. Combine stock, oyster sauce, cornstarch, chili paste, and sesame oil in small saucepan. Stir well and set aside.
3. Cut white portion of scallions into 2-inch pieces. Chop enough of green portion to make 1 tablespoon. Set aside separately.
4. Combine ginger, white scallion pieces, and hot red peppers.
5. In small bowl, combine brown sugar, mushroom soy sauce, and ginger wine or dry sherry. Set aside.
6. Heat oil in wok or heavy skillet until hot. Place fish in pan and brown about 3 minutes. As fish steaks are browning, sprinkle ginger, red pepper, and white part of scallions over them.
7. Turn fish and fry other side 3 minutes.
8. Remove pan from heat and carefully pour off all but 1 tablespoon of the oil and return pan to stove. Continue to brown fish steaks and sprinkle over them the sugar and soy sauce mixture.
9. Over medium-high heat, bring oyster sauce mixture to a boil, stirring constantly. Continue to cook until sauce just begins to thicken, or until fish flakes when gently touched with a fork.
10. Quickly pour sauce over fish and let simmer about 3 minutes.
11. Remove fish with sauce to serving plate. Garnish with the tablespoon of chopped scallion greens.

Pink Chinese Radishes
Spicy Fried Calf's Liver
Mountain Snow White Chicken/Rice

Snowy white chicken with snow peas, rich brown calf's liver and radishes, combined with rice and tea, satisfy big appetites.

Set the table with brightly colored serving pieces to highlight this elegant meal.

Besides being rich in texture, color, and flavor, this meal is nutritionally rich as well: it contains calf's liver, chicken, rice, and several vegetables. Select liver that is pale and odorless, and before cooking it, remove membranes to prevent the liver from curling up when cooked.

Your shopping list for this menu includes two essential Chinese ingredients—oyster sauce and chili paste. Oyster sauce is a typical Cantonese condiment. It has a rich, salty, rather strong oyster taste and is used frequently to flavor stir fries and as a condiment at the table. After opening, oyster sauce should be stored in the refrigerator, where it will last indefinitely. Chili paste, sold in jars, is made from fresh ground red chilies, garlic, and other spices. Because this paste is very hot, use it sparingly in cooking or serve it as a condiment. This, too, should be stored in the refrigerator. There are no substitutes for either of these.

Mushroom soy sauce, on the other hand, is good to have as an option. Delicately flavored with mushrooms and saltier than standard light soy sauces, mushroom soy sauce tastes delicious in stir fries. Unfortunately it is difficult to find, but you will not harm the recipe if you use regular soy sauce instead.

Ginger wine, a flavoring ingredient for the calf's liver marinade, is easily made by soaking four to five ounces of peeled, minced fresh ginger in Chinese rice wine. In a few days, the wine is ready to use. This wine lasts indefinitely when stored in the refrigerator.

If you cannot find long, white Chinese radishes, use the small red Western ones. And when sugar snap peas are not in season, use snow peas, which are usually in the market year round. Straw mushrooms, which have a silken texture and a very delicate taste, are often used in stir-fried dishes and soups. If you have access to a Chinese produce market, ask for fresh straw mushrooms, which are small and brown, and take their name from the straw on which they grow. Fresh straw mushrooms are difficult to find; the canned ones are more readily available in well-stocked supermarkets or Oriental stores. Fresh ones will keep three to four days in the refrigerator, and the canned ones will keep for a week after opening, provided you store them in a covered container.

WHAT TO DRINK

Here again the flavors of the dishes are not really compatible with wine, so serve beer, ale, or tea.

SHOPPING LIST AND STAPLES

1½ pounds skinless, boneless chicken breasts (about 2 whole breasts)
1 pound calf's liver
1 pound radishes, preferably Chinese white variety, or Western red
12 sugar snap peas, preferably, or snow peas
1 bunch scallions
1 small onion
Fresh ginger
4 cloves garlic
1 egg
½ cup Chinese Chicken Stock (see page 13)
15-ounce can straw mushrooms
1 teaspoon oyster sauce
4 cups plus 2 tablespoons peanut or vegetable oil
1½ teaspoons sesame oil
¼ cup light soy sauce plus 1 teaspoon (optional)
1 teaspoon mushroom soy sauce (optional)
3 tablespoons white distilled vinegar
2 teaspoons wine vinegar
½ teaspoon chili paste
1 cup uncooked rice
½ cup plus 1 tablespoon plus 1½ teaspoons cornstarch
¼ teaspoon baking soda
3 tablespoons plus ¼ teaspoon sugar
Salt and black pepper
2 tablespoons ginger wine, preferably, or dry sherry
1 tablespoon dry white wine

UTENSILS

Wok
    or Dutch oven (for calf's liver)
    and heavy 12-inch skillet (for chicken)
3-quart saucepan
Medium-size saucepan with cover (for rice)
Small plate
2 medium-size bowls
4 small bowls
Measuring cups and spoons
Chinese cleaver or chef's knife
Paring knife
Chinese mesh spoon or long-handled slotted metal spoon
16-inch chopsticks or long-handled wooden spoon
Deep-fat thermometer

1. Follow pink radishes recipe, steps 1 and 2.
2. Follow general rice recipe on page 12, steps 1 and 2.
3. Follow fried calf's liver recipe step 1. Lightly beat egg white for chicken and follow snow white chicken recipe steps 1 and 2.
4. Preheat oven to 200 degrees and follow pink radishes recipe step 3.
5. Follow fried calf's liver recipe steps 2 through 5.
6. Wipe out wok. Follow general rice recipe step 3.
7. Complete snow white chicken dish, steps 3 through 10, fried calf's liver recipe step 6, pink radishes recipe step 4, and rice recipe step 4. Serve.

RECIPES

Pink Chinese Radishes

1 pound radishes, preferably Chinese white variety, or Western red
¾ teaspoon salt
3 tablespoons white distilled vinegar
3 tablespoons sugar

1. Cut radishes in half lengthwise, then slice crosswise into thin slices.
2. Combine radish slices and salt in small bowl. Mix thoroughly and let stand 15 minutes.
3. Drain off any salty water and add vinegar and sugar. Mix thoroughly and let stand 10 minutes.
4. When ready to serve, drain juice and place radishes around the fried liver.

Spicy Fried Calf's Liver

1 pound calf's liver
1 teaspoon mushroom soy sauce or light soy sauce
1 tablespoon ginger wine, preferably, or dry sherry
⅛ teaspoon black pepper

The sauce:
1 scallion, including top, thinly sliced
½ teaspoon sesame oil
¼ teaspoon sugar
¼ cup light soy sauce
1 teaspoon oyster sauce
3 cloves garlic, minced
2 teaspoons wine vinegar
½ teaspoon chili paste

4 cups peanut or vegetable oil
½ cup cornstarch

1. Cut liver into small serving pieces. Rinse, pat dry with paper towels, and place in medium-size bowl. Add mushroom or light soy sauce, ginger wine, and black pepper. Mix thoroughly. Let stand 10 minutes or longer.
2. In small bowl, stir to combine sauce ingredients.
3. Heat oil in wok or Dutch oven over medium-high heat to 375 degrees on deep-fat thermometer. Put cornstarch on small plate.

4. Dust marinated liver with cornstarch, making sure that all pieces are evenly but lightly coated.
5. When oil is very hot, carefully add half the liver pieces and cook about 1 to 2 minutes. Remove from oil with Chinese mesh spoon or long-handled slotted metal spoon and place on heatproof serving platter lined with paper towels to drain. Keep warm in preheated 200-degree oven while you cook remaining half.
6. When ready to serve, pour sauce over liver and garnish with radishes.

Mountain Snow White Chicken

1½ pounds skinless, boneless chicken breasts (about 2 whole breasts)

The marinade:
1 tablespoon cornstarch
¼ teaspoon baking soda
1 tablespoon vegetable oil
1 tablespoon dry white wine
1 egg white, lightly beaten
Pinch salt

The sauce:
½ cup Chinese Chicken Stock
1 tablespoon ginger wine, preferably, or dry sherry
1 teaspoon sesame oil
1½ teaspoons cornstarch
12 sugar snap peas, preferably, or snow peas
16 straw mushrooms (about ½ can)
1 tablespoon peanut or vegetable oil
½ teaspoon minced ginger
½ teaspoon minced garlic
1 tablespoon minced onion

1. Slice chicken into pieces about 3 inches long, 1 inch wide, and ¼ inch thick, or into long slices.
2. Combine marinade ingredients in medium-size mixing bowl. Add chicken and mix thoroughly to coat well. Let stand 10 minutes or longer.
3. Bring 2 quarts water to a boil in 3-quart saucepan.
4. Combine sauce ingredients in small bowl, stirring to dissolve cornstarch.
5. Rinse sugar snap peas and pull off strings. Set aside in small bowl with straw mushrooms.
6. Add marinated chicken to the boiling water and cook, stirring, until chicken begins to turn white, about 1 minute. Pour chicken into colander and drain well.
7. Heat cooking oil in wok or large, heavy skillet. When oil is hot, add ginger, garlic, and onion, and using 16-inch chopsticks or wooden spoon, stir fry a few seconds.
8. Add straw mushrooms and sugar snap peas, and stir fry 30 seconds.
9. Stir sauce once more and add to pan. Add blanched chicken and bring sauce to a boil, stirring constantly until sauce begins to thicken.
10. Remove from heat and place chicken on heated serving plate.

Vegetable Balls with Sweet and Sour Sauce
Spicy Lamb with Tree Ear Mushrooms
Sautéed Shrimp with Cucumbers / Rice

An attractive way to present this meal is in individual un-matched serving pieces, that underline the contrasting colors *of the pale orange shrimp, the golden vegetable balls, and the brown spicy lamb.*

As a child, Jeri Sipe helped prepare this recipe for vegetable balls as part of an annual family feast. She recalls picking the vegetables—cabbage, onions, carrots, and water chestnuts—in the fields, then making the vegetable balls with her mother. The sweet and sour dipping sauce that accompanies them here is thought to have originated in Canton.

Lamb, a Mongolian favorite, has always been more popular in northern than in southern China, but centuries ago almost all Chinese considered lamb unfit for civilized people. The reason: its strong aroma. Although attitudes have changed, lamb is still not readily available in southern China. Whenever this meat is used, regardless of the region, Chinese cooks generally slice or shred it and camouflage it with strong ingredients. For this recipe, Jeri Sipe calls for a boned lamb shoulder, cut into pieces, which are then marinated in ginger wine, mushroom soy sauce, cinnamon, and sesame oil. The dried tree ear mushrooms that accompany the lamb look like crumpled scorched paper, but soaking restores them to their original size. For appearance as for flavor, there are no direct Western mushroom equivalents, but you could use a dried European mushroom.

WHAT TO DRINK

A well-chilled Soave or similar dry, fruity white wine, or a California Semillon or Emerald Riesling can accompany these dishes.

SHOPPING LIST AND STAPLES

1 pound boneless lamb shoulder
¾ pound medium-size fresh shrimp
1 head cabbage
1 medium-size cucumber
1 bunch scallions
2 small onions
1 carrot
1 small red bell pepper
4 hot red peppers
¾ ounce dried tree ear mushrooms (about 10)
Fresh ginger
1 clove garlic
1 egg
½ cup Chinese Chicken Stock (see page 13) or fish broth
¼ cup beef broth
8-ounce can water chestnuts
1 tablespoon plus 2 teaspoons oyster sauce
4 cups plus 4 tablespoons peanut or vegetable oil
2¼ teaspoons sesame oil
1 tablespoon mushroom soy sauce, preferably, or light soy sauce
1½ tablespoons catsup
Worcestershire sauce
2 tablespoons white or Chinese dark vinegar
1 cup uncooked rice
¼ cup flour

2 tablespoons plus 4 teaspoons cornstarch
½ teaspoon baking powder
⅝ teaspoon baking soda
2 tablespoons plus ½ teaspoon sugar
Cinnamon
Salt and black pepper
¼ teaspoon Cayenne pepper
1 tablespoon ginger wine or dry sherry
2 tablespoons dry white wine

UTENSILS

Food processor (optional)
Wok
    or heavy 12-inch skillet (for vegetable balls; lamb)
2 medium-size saucepans, 1 with cover (for rice)
Small saucepan with cover
Heatproof plate
2 large mixing bowls
Medium-size bowl
4 small bowls
Metal colander
Measuring cups and spoons
Chinese cleaver or chef's knife
Paring knife
Chinese mesh spoon or long-handled slotted metal spoon
16-inch chopsticks or long-handled wooden spoon
Vegetable peeler
Deep-fat thermometer
Small scissors, preferably embroidery type

START-TO-FINISH STEPS

1. Follow spicy lamb recipe steps 1 through 3.
2. Follow general rice recipe on page 12, steps 1 and 2.
3. Follow vegetable balls recipe steps 1 and 2.
4. Follow sautéed shrimp recipe steps 1 through 6.
5. Preheat oven to 200 degrees. Follow spicy lamb recipe steps 4 through 11.
6. Wipe out pan. Follow vegetable balls recipe steps 3 through 5 and general rice recipe step 3.
7. Wipe out pan very well. Complete sautéed shrimp recipe, steps 7 and 8.
8. Present dipping sauces for vegetable balls, step 6, follow general rice recipe, step 4, and serve the hot food immediately. Be sure to remove hot red peppers from lamb dish before serving.

RECIPES

Vegetable Balls with Sweet and Sour Sauce

1 small onion (about ¼ pound)
¼ head cabbage, coarsely chopped
½ carrot, trimmed and peeled
12 to 16 water chestnuts
1 teaspoon peanut or vegetable oil
¼ cup flour
1 tablespoon plus 2 teaspoons cornstarch
1 egg, beaten

74

¼ teaspoon baking soda
½ teaspoon baking powder
Black pepper
2 tablespoons plus ½ teaspoon sugar
¼ teaspoon salt
4 cups peanut or vegetable oil
½ cup water
2 tablespoons white or Chinese dark vinegar
1½ tablespoons catsup

1. Mince onion, cabbage, carrot, and water chestnuts in food processor fitted with steel blade or with sharp knife. Combine vegetables, 1 teaspoon oil, flour, and 1 teaspoon cornstarch in large mixing bowl. Add half the beaten egg and combine thoroughly.
2. Add baking soda, baking powder, dash of black pepper, ½ teaspoon sugar, and salt. Mix thoroughly.
3. Heat 4 cups oil in wok or large heavy skillet to 375 degrees on deep-fat thermometer.
4. For the sauce, dissolve remaining cornstarch in the water in small saucepan and add vinegar, sugar, and catsup. Bring sauce to a boil and cook until it begins to thicken. Turn off heat. Cover pan and set aside.
5. Shape vegetable mixture into small patties or, using a small spoon dipped in water, form walnut-size balls. Gently drop them into the hot oil until there is 1 layer. Fry until golden brown on all sides. Remove with Chinese mesh spoon or long-handled slotted metal spoon and drain on heatproof plate lined with paper towels. Repeat until all the vegetable balls have been cooked. Keep warm in preheated 200-degree oven.
6. Place sweet and sour sauce in bowl and serve as a dip for the vegetable balls.

Spicy Lamb with Tree Ear Mushrooms

¾ ounce dried tree ear mushrooms (about 10)

The marinade:
1 tablespoon ginger wine or dry sherry
1 tablespoon mushroom soy sauce, preferably, or light soy sauce
¼ teaspoon baking soda
Dash of cinnamon
1½ teaspoons sesame oil

1 pound boneless lamb shoulder

The sauce:
1 tablespoon oyster sauce
1 teaspoon cornstarch
½ teaspoon Worcestershire sauce
¼ cup beef broth or water

3 scallions, including tops, cut in 2-inch lengths
4 hot red peppers
1 teaspoon minced garlic
2 teaspoons minced fresh ginger
1 small red bell pepper, cored, seeded, and sliced thin
2 tablespoons peanut or vegetable oil

1. In small bowl, cover mushrooms with boiling water and allow to soak about 15 to 20 minutes.

2. Combine marinade ingredients in large mixing bowl.
3. Slice lamb horizontally into ⅛-inch thick pieces, and then cut into 3-inch squares. Add lamb to marinade and mix thoroughly.
4. Combine sauce ingredients in small bowl. Stir well to dissolve cornstarch.
5. Rinse tree ears under running water. Cut off and discard stems. Cut tree ears into ¼-inch strips.
6. Place white parts of scallions in small bowl with hot red peppers, garlic, and ginger. Add cut green tops to the tree ears.
7. Heat wok or skillet. Add oil and heat until very hot. Add ginger and scallion mixture. Stir fry about 5 seconds.
8. Add lamb and marinade and stir constantly 1 minute.
9. Add tree ears, scallion greens, and red bell pepper strips. Stir fry until tree ears are heated through.
10. Stir sauce once more and add to pan. Mix thoroughly and cook, stirring, until sauce begins to thicken.
11. Pour contents into heated serving dish and keep warm in oven. Remove the hot red peppers before serving.

Sautéed Shrimp with Cucumbers

¾ pound medium-size fresh shrimp
⅛ teaspoon baking soda
1 tablespoon cornstarch
Pinch of salt

The sauce:
½ cup Chinese Chicken Stock or fish broth
1 teaspoon cornstarch
2 teaspoons oyster sauce
¾ teaspoon sesame oil

1 medium-size cucumber
½ carrot, peeled and sliced thin
2 tablespoons peanut or vegetable oil
½ small onion, sliced thin
3 quarter-size slices fresh ginger
¼ teaspoon Cayenne pepper
2 tablespoons dry white wine

1. Shell and devein shrimp by cutting a slit along backs. Rinse under cold running water and pat dry with paper towels.
2. Combine baking soda, cornstarch, and salt in medium-size bowl and add shrimp, tossing to mix well.
3. Bring 1 quart water to a boil in medium-size saucepan for blanching shrimp.
4. Combine sauce ingredients in small bowl.
5. Peel cucumber and slice it in half lengthwise. Scoop out seeds and cut cucumber crosswise into ¼-inch slices.
6. Blanch shrimp 20 seconds and drain in colander.
7. Heat peanut oil in wok or skillet over medium heat. Add onion, ginger, and Cayenne pepper, and stir fry 5 seconds. Add cucumber and carrot slices and stir fry 20 seconds. Add wine and shrimp, and stir constantly 1 minute.
8. Stir sauce once more and pour over shrimp. Cook, stirring constantly, until sauce is heated through. Pour shrimp and sauce onto heated serving plate.

Ken Hom

MENU 1 (Left)
Chicken Thighs with Garlic, Scallion,
and Vinegar Sauce
Stir-Fried Squash with Szechwan Peppercorns
Fried Rice with Ham, Egg, and Peas

MENU 2
Cauliflower with Hoisin Sauce
Crisp Chicken Strips
with Black-Bean Orange Sauce
Stir-Fried Cucumbers with Tomatoes and Garlic
Rice

MENU 3
Chicken and Watercress Soup
Steamed Fish with Ginger, Scallions,
and Coriander
Glazed Carrots with Oyster Sauce
Rice

Ken Hom, born in Arizona and now based in California, learned to cook twenty-two years ago in his uncle's Chinese restaurant in Chicago. Most of the chefs there came from Hong Kong, and Ken Hom still relies on the Southern Chinese tastes and techniques that he learned in his early training. But he also had the chance to serve as an apprentice to cooks from other regions—Shanghai, Peking, and the western provinces of Szechwan and Hunan—who were specialists in highly spiced foods long before most restaurants here began serving them.

From his Chicago experience, Ken Hom also learned the virtues of improvisation. Following recipes to the letter, he says, is not nearly as important as starting with fresh ingredients. If a recipe calls for fish and you cannot find any fresh fish, you are better off substituting boned chicken breasts than using frozen fish. If a recipe calls for special ingredients that are impossible to find, use something else. Above all, trust your instincts.

The three menus here achieve classic Chinese tastes with familiar Western ingredients. Menu 2 features cauliflower, a vegetable not even available in China. Menus 1 and 3 have the abundance of vegetables typical of Cantonese cooking. Common to these three meals is a range of contrasting textures.

In this satisfying meal, the colors of the squash and peppers add a festive note. A green or yellow platter for the fried rice will pick up the colors of the scrambled eggs or the green peas. The chicken thighs look appetizing on a bed of lettuce.

Chicken Thighs with Garlic, Scallion, and Vinegar Sauce
Stir-Fried Squash with Szechwan Peppercorns
Fried Rice with Ham, Egg, and Peas

This meal of chicken thighs, stir-fried squash, and fried rice is ideal family fare. The garlic-laden chicken thighs are the star attraction, a spicy dish to accompany the milder fried rice. Garlic is a Chinese favorite, and in this dish, it is spooned over the chicken in a soy and vinegar sauce.

Szechwan peppercorns, unlike the familiar black peppercorns, are tiny reddish-brown kernels covered with a husk. They taste mildly hot and have a pungent aroma. To heighten their flavor, cook the peppercorns for a few moments in an ungreased pan over a medium flame. Shake the pan frequently so that the kernels do not burn. When they have released their aromatic oil, remove them from the heat and allow them to cool slightly. Then grind them in a blender or coffee mill. Store the unused portion in a tightly covered jar.

The crushed peppercorns are used to season the stir-fried vegetables. Zucchini and yellow squash are most plentiful in the summer but are nonetheless available all year. For the tenderest squash, buy those that are less than eight inches long. Sweet red bell peppers should be firm and shiny.

A platter of fried rice is a Cantonese specialty; indeed, it can easily be a meal in itself. In making fried rice, which is a staple of home-style cooking, you can be flexible about what you add to the dish. Before stir frying, start with cold and firm cooked rice so that the grains will stay separate when you do stir fry. Ham, eggs, and peas are the ingredients in this recipe, but you may also add nuts, cooked cubed chicken, cooked shrimp, mushrooms—or almost any good leftover vegetables or meats. The eggs, of course, are as essential as the rice, and peas or a green vegetable add a pleasing color.

WHAT TO DRINK

Because of the prominence of the garlic and the peppercorns, beer would go especially well with this meal. However, if you are interested in experimenting, this menu provides an opportunity to match a red wine with Chinese food: first preference would be a light, fresh wine, like a Beaujolais or an inexpensive California zinfandel.

SHOPPING LIST AND STAPLES

3 pounds chicken thighs
4 ounces prosciutto or Smithfield ham, in one piece
¾ pound yellow squash (about 2 medium size)
¾ pound zucchini (about 2 medium size)
2 red bell peppers
1 pound fresh peas
1 bunch scallions
1 small head curly endive or Boston lettuce (optional)
6 cloves garlic
4 large eggs
4 cups plus 7 tablespoons peanut oil
1 teaspoon Oriental sesame oil
4 tablespoons light soy sauce
4 tablespoons Chinese red rice vinegar, or 3 tablespoons
   Western red wine vinegar
2½ cups uncooked rice
Salt
1 teaspoon Szechwan peppercorns

UTENSILS

Blender
Wok
   or Dutch oven (for completing chicken)
   and 12-inch skillet with cover (for steaming chicken) plus
      heavy 12-inch skillet (for squash; fried rice)
   and small skillet (for cooking peppercorns)
Medium-size saucepan with cover (for rice)
Small saucepan
Heatproof platter (for steaming)
Small plate
3 small bowls
Metal trivet or rack (for steaming)
Metal colander
Measuring cups and spoons
Chinese cleaver or chef's knife
Metal wok spatula or 2 long-handled wooden spoons
Chinese mesh spoon or long-handled slotted metal spoon
2 chopsticks
Deep-fat thermometer

START-TO-FINISH STEPS

1. Follow general rice recipe on page 12, steps 1 and 2.
2. Follow chicken recipe steps 1 and 2.
3. Mince the scallions and garlic for chicken recipe and follow step 3.
4. Trim prosciutto or ham and follow fried rice recipe steps 1 through 4.

5. Follow stir-fried squash recipe step 1.
6. Follow fried rice recipe step 5.
7. Follow stir-fried squash recipe step 2.
8. Follow chicken recipe steps 4 through 6.
9. Follow general rice recipe step 3 and fried rice recipe steps 6 and 7. Remove to heatproof serving platter and keep warm.
10. Wipe out pan. Follow chicken recipe steps 7 and 8.
11. Wipe out pan. Follow stir-fried squash recipe steps 3 through 5.
12. Remove stir-fried rice and chicken from oven. Garnish chicken recipe as in step 9 and serve everything at once.

___

RECIPES

Chicken Thighs with Garlic, Scallion, and Vinegar Sauce

3 pounds chicken thighs
4 cups peanut oil
½ cup finely minced scallion
3 tablespoons minced garlic (about 6 cloves)
4 tablespoons Chinese red rice vinegar, or 3 tablespoons Western red wine vinegar
4 tablespoons light soy sauce
Curly endive or Boston lettuce for garnish (optional)

1. Bring 1 inch of water to a boil in wok or in large skillet.
2. Place chicken on heatproof platter and set on metal trivet or rack to steam, covered, 20 minutes.
3. Combine scallion, garlic, vinegar, and soy sauce in small bowl.
4. Preheat oven to 200 degrees.
5. Heat wok or Dutch oven, add oil, and heat to 375 degrees on deep-fat thermometer or until a scallion ring sizzles on contact.
6. Remove chicken from steamer and blot any moisture on the thighs with paper towels.
7. Gently add half the chicken pieces to the hot oil and deep fry until crisp and brown, about 10 minutes.
8. Remove chicken thighs with Chinese mesh spoon or long-handled slotted metal spoon and briefly hold them above pan to drain off excess oil. Arrange them on large platter and keep warm in oven. Return oil to 375 degrees and cook second batch. Keep warm in oven.
9. Serve chicken on bed of lettuce, if desired, and spoon over some of the vinegar sauce. Serve remaining sauce separately.

Stir-Fried Squash with Szechwan Peppercorns

1 teaspoon Szechwan peppercorns
¾ pound yellow squash (about 2 medium size)
¾ pound zucchini (about 2 medium size)
2 red bell peppers, seeded and cored
3 tablespoons peanut oil
2 teaspoons salt

1. Cook peppercorns in dry wok or small skillet over medium heat about 1 minute. Spin them in blender only until crushed and set aside.
2. Thinly slice squash on the bias. Slice peppers into thin strips.
3. Heat wok until it takes on a rainbowlike shimmer or heat large, heavy skillet. Add peanut oil.
4. When oil is almost smoking, add salt and sliced squash. Stir fry quickly over high heat, then immediately add red peppers. Stir fry until vegetables are slightly wilted, about 3 minutes.
5. Stir in crushed peppercorns and toss well to combine. Spoon onto serving platter and keep warm.

Fried Rice with Ham, Egg, and Peas

4 ounces prosciutto or Smithfield ham, in one piece, and trimmed of fat
4 large eggs
1 teaspoon sesame oil
1 teaspoon salt
1 cup fresh peas, shelled
4 tablespoons peanut oil
5 to 6 cups cooked rice, at room temperature

1. Cut ham into ¼-inch cubes.
2. Bring ½ cup water to a boil in small saucepan.
3. Beat eggs with chopsticks or a fork and add sesame oil and salt.
4. Cook peas in boiling water 3 minutes. Drain in colander.
5. Heat large heavy skillet until almost smoking. Add 1 tablespoon of the oil. Add egg mixture and stir fry until partially "set" in one piece. Turn out onto small plate and slice into thin strips. Set aside.
6. Wipe out pan with paper towels and reheat. Add remaining 3 tablespoons oil. When almost smoking, add rice and ham. Cook, stirring constantly to prevent sticking, about 5 minutes, or until rice is thoroughly heated.
7. Add cooked eggs and peas, and heat, stirring, 3 to 5 minutes. Taste for seasoning.

Cauliflower with Hoisin Sauce
Crisp Chicken Strips with Black-Bean Orange Sauce
Stir-Fried Cucumbers with Tomatoes and Garlic / Rice

Crisp strips of chicken and cauliflower flowerets glazed with hoisin sauce provide a pretty color contrast to the stir-fried cucumbers with tomatoes and garlic. Use informal pottery for this appealing one-plate meal.

The rich, spicy *hoisin* sauce adds a pleasant nutty color and brings out the slightly cabbagey taste of crisp-cooked cauliflower in the first dish of this menu.

The stir-fried chicken has a sauce flavored with salted black beans, garlic, and orange juice. Salted black beans are soybeans that have been boiled and then soaked in brine for six months.

The zest of an orange is its outer skin, shaved off without the underlying white rind. When you mince or grate the zest, the oils in it will release a wonderful fragrance.

WHAT TO DRINK

Serve a robustly flavored tea such as China Green or Keemun or, if you want wine, a California Chenin Blanc.

SHOPPING LIST AND STAPLES

1½ to 2 pounds skinless, boneless chicken breasts
1 head cauliflower (about 1½ pounds)
4 large tomatoes (about 1½ pounds)
3 large cucumbers (about 1½ pounds)
1 orange
1 bunch scallions

2 tablespoons Chinese salted black beans
4 large shallots
12 cloves garlic
2 eggs
½ cup Chinese Chicken Stock (see page 13)
6 tablespoons *hoisin* sauce
4 cups plus 4 tablespoons peanut oil
1 tablespoon Oriental sesame oil
2 tablespoons dark soy sauce
¾ cup unbleached flour
¾ cup plus 1 tablespoon cornstarch
2 tablespoons plus ½ teaspoon sugar
Salt
1 tablespoon Chinese rice wine or dry sherry

UTENSILS

Wok
   or Dutch oven (for chicken)
   and heavy 12-inch skillet with cover (for completing
      chicken; cucumbers)
Large saucepan
Heatproof serving platter
3 medium-size bowls

Small bowl
Metal colander
Measuring cups and spoons
Chinese cleaver or chef's knife
Paring knife
Metal wok spatula or 2 long-handled wooden spoons
Chinese mesh spoon or long-handled slotted metal spoon
Citrus juicer and zester
Deep-fat thermometer

START-TO-FINISH STEPS

1. Follow chicken recipe step 1. Preheat oven to 200 degrees.
2. Follow stir-fried cucumbers recipe step 1.
3. Follow chicken recipe steps 2 through 5.
4. Trim cauliflower into flowerets, mince scallions, and follow cauliflower recipe steps 1 through 3.
5. Follow stir-fried cucumbers recipe steps 2 and 3.
6. Follow chicken recipe steps 6 and 7.
7. Follow cauliflower recipe step 4. Keep cauliflower warm in oven while you cook the cucumbers.
8. Wipe out pan. Follow stir-fried cucumbers recipe steps 4 through 6. Remove chicken from oven and follow step 8. Remove cauliflower from oven and serve.

RECIPES

Cauliflower with Hoisin Sauce

1 tablespoon salt
1 head cauliflower (about 1½ pounds)
6 tablespoons *hoisin* sauce
1 tablespoon sesame oil
3 tablespoons minced scallions

1. Bring 2 cups water to a boil in large saucepan. Add salt and blanch cauliflower 5 minutes.
2. Mix remaining ingredients in small bowl.
3. Drain cauliflower in colander and let cool 5 minutes.
4. Turn into a serving bowl and toss with sauce mixture.

Crisp Chicken Strips with Black-Bean Orange Sauce

The chicken and marinade:
1½ to 2 pounds skinless, boneless chicken breasts
2 eggs
2 tablespoons peanut oil
2 tablespoons dark soy sauce
1 tablespoon Chinese rice wine or dry sherry
½ teaspoon sugar

The deep frying:
4 cups peanut oil
½ to ¾ cup unbleached flour
½ to ¾ cup cornstarch

The sauce:
2 tablespoons peanut oil
2 tablespoons Chinese salted black beans
2 tablespoons minced garlic (about 6 cloves)
½ cup Chinese Chicken Stock

¼ cup freshly squeezed orange juice
1 tablespoon cornstarch dissolved in 3 tablespoons water
1 teaspoon Chinese sesame oil
Orange zest for garnish (optional)

1. Cut chicken into long strips about 1 inch wide. Combine marinade ingredients in medium-size bowl and blend well. Add chicken strips, tossing to coat them with marinade.
2. Heat peanut oil in wok or Dutch oven to 375 degrees on deep-fat thermometer or until a sliver of garlic sizzles.
3. Combine flour and cornstarch in medium-size bowl. Coat chicken strips in the mixture, shaking off any excess.
4. Deep fry the strips in two batches until they are golden brown, about 3 to 5 minutes. Remove them with Chinese mesh spoon or long-handled slotted metal spoon and drain them over pan. Place on platter lined with paper towels and keep warm in oven.
5. Drain wok, if used, and wipe out with paper towels.
6. For the sauce, heat wok until it takes on a rainbowlike shimmer or heat large heavy skillet until almost smoking. Add 2 tablespoons peanut oil, then black beans and garlic. Stir fry 30 seconds.
7. Add chicken stock and orange juice, and bring to a boil. Stir in cornstarch mixture and cook, stirring constantly, until thickened and bubbling. Add sesame oil and remove from heat. Pour sauce into serving bowl.
8. Pour a little of the sauce over the chicken strips and garnish with orange zest, if desired. Serve remaining sauce on the side.

Stir-Fried Cucumbers with Tomatoes and Garlic

3 large cucumbers (about 1½ pounds)
2 teaspoons salt
4 large tomatoes (about 1½ pounds)
2 tablespoons sugar
2 tablespoons peanut oil
3 tablespoons minced shallots
2 tablespoons minced garlic (about 6 cloves)
2 teaspoons sesame oil

1. Peel cucumbers and cut in half lengthwise. Scoop out seeds with teaspoon. Cut cucumber halves into long strips, then crosswise into 1-inch pieces. Put in colander and sprinkle with 1 teaspoon of salt.
2. Bring 4 cups water to a boil in large saucepan. Blanch tomatoes, 2 at a time, 10 seconds. Peel, seed, and chop tomatoes. Put in medium-size bowl and sprinkle with sugar.
3. Remove cucumbers and blot with linen kitchen towel or paper towels. Drain chopped tomatoes in colander.
4. Heat wok until it takes on a rainbowlike shimmer or heat large heavy skillet and add peanut oil.
5. Add cucumber to the hot oil and stir to coat. Add shallots, garlic, remaining 1 teaspoon salt and sesame oil. Stir fry 3 minutes.
6. Add tomatoes and toss just to warm, about 1 minute. Serve immediately.

Chicken and Watercress Soup
Steamed Fish with Ginger, Scallions, and Coriander
Glazed Carrots with Oyster Sauce / Rice

You can serve this informal meal in the various cooking containers—a wok, a bamboo steamer, and a copper soup pot.

This light, nutritious meal of soup, steamed fish, glazed carrots, and rice makes a fine warm-weather luncheon or dinner. The delicate homemade chicken soup is flavored with a whole chicken that is later strained from the broth. To prepare the stock Western-style, disjoint the chicken and add the pieces to the boiling water. Or, you may prepare the stock by the authentic Chinese method of cleaving the chicken into two-inch pieces, which exposes more chicken surface and produces a richer chicken flavor. The watercress will add its good tart flavor. You put the fresh leaves in the soup bowl—not in the pot—and pour the broth over them. This gently blanches and wilts the watercress but does not overcook it.

Use any of the fish the recipe calls for as long as it is fresh. The carrots provide an unusual flavor when combined with the oyster sauce.

WHAT TO DRINK

Because of its simplicity, this menu will accommodate a dry, relatively full-bodied white wine, such as a moderately priced California or New York Chardonnay.

SHOPPING LIST AND STAPLES

4 fresh halibut or sea bass, red snapper, or mako shark steaks (about 1½ pounds)
2½-pound whole chicken
¾ to 1 pound skinless, boneless chicken breasts

2 pounds baby carrots
2 bunches watercress
1 large bunch scallions
1 bunch coriander
Fresh ginger
2 cloves garlic
2 tablespoons oyster sauce
2½ tablespoons peanut oil
1 cup uncooked rice
Salt and freshly ground pepper

UTENSILS

Stockpot or kettle with cover
Wok with cover
    or heavy 12-inch skillet (for carrots)
    and bamboo steamer (for fish)
    and small roasting pan (for fish)
Medium-size saucepan with cover (for rice)
Small saucepan
Heatproof platter
Heatproof plate
Large bowl
Metal trivet
Sieve
Measuring cups and spoons
Heavy Chinese cleaver or chef's knife
Chinese mesh spoon or long-handled slotted metal spoon
2 long-handled wooden spoons

Vegetable peeler
Cheesecloth

START-TO-FINISH STEPS

1. Follow chicken soup recipe steps 1 through 3.
2. Preheat oven to 200 degrees. Follow glazed carrots recipe step 1.
3. Follow chicken soup recipe steps 4 and 5.
4. Slice ginger for chicken soup recipe; mince ginger for steamed fish recipe. Follow general rice recipe on page 12, steps 1 and 2.
5. Follow steamed fish recipe steps 1 through 3.
6. Follow glazed carrots recipe step 2.
7. Follow rice recipe step 3 and chicken soup recipe step 6.
8. Follow glazed carrots recipe step 3.
9. Follow chicken soup recipe steps 7 and 8, steamed fish recipe step 4, rice recipe step 4, and serve.

RECIPES

Chicken and Watercress Soup

2½-pound whole chicken
¾ to 1 pound skinless, boneless chicken breasts
4 quarter-size slices fresh ginger
4 scallions, white part only
Salt
2 cups loosely packed fresh watercress leaves

1. Bring 8 cups water to a boil in stockpot or kettle.
2. Using heavy cleaver or knife, disjoint whole chicken or, to prepare Chinese style, chop into 2-inch pieces.
3. Separately, cut boneless chicken breasts into short, thin strips.
4. Blanch chicken breast strips in the boiling water 1 minute. Remove with Chinese mesh spoon or slotted metal spoon to heatproof plate and keep warm in preheated 200-degree oven.
5. Add the cut-up chicken to the boiling water. Turn down heat and skim off any scum that forms on surface. Add ginger, scallions, and salt to taste, and simmer, uncovered, about 30 minutes, skimming from time to time. The broth should be reduced by half.
6. Ten minutes before serving, strain broth through sieve lined with cheesecloth into large bowl to remove chicken pieces, ginger, and scallions used for flavoring. Rinse out pot. Using your spoon or a triple layer of paper toweling

gently draped across the surface, remove surface fat from broth. Reserve 1 cup for glazed carrots.
7. Return remaining broth and blanched chicken strips to pot. Reheat and add salt if necessary.
8. Place handful of watercress leaves into each of four soup bowls. Ladle hot broth and chicken pieces into the bowls.

Steamed Fish with Ginger, Scallions, and Coriander

4 fresh halibut or sea bass, red snapper, or mako shark
    steaks (about 1½ pounds)
Salt and freshly ground pepper
1 tablespoon minced scallions
1 tablespoon minced coriander
1 teaspoon minced fresh ginger
1½ tablespoons peanut oil

1. Bring 1 inch of water to a boil in wok or small roasting pan. (For bamboo steaming method, see page 13.)
2. Place fish steaks on heatproof platter and set on rack or metal trivet. Sprinkle fish with salt and pepper, and scatter scallions, coriander, and ginger over them.
3. If using wok, cover with wok lid. If using roasting pan, cover tightly with double-strength aluminum foil. Steam fish steaks 8 to 12 minutes, depending on their thickness, or until done. Be careful of the hot steam, particularly if you are lifting up tent of aluminum foil.
4. Just before serving, heat peanut oil in small saucepan. Drizzle over the steamed fish.

Glazed Carrots with Oyster Sauce

2 pounds baby carrots
1 tablespoon peanut oil
2 cloves garlic, peeled and lightly crushed
1 cup reserved chicken broth from soup recipe
    or canned broth
2 tablespoons oyster sauce

1. Peel carrots and roll cut them (see page 10).
2. Heat wok until it has a rainbowlike shimmer or heat large, heavy skillet until almost smoking and add peanut oil. Add carrots and crushed garlic. Stir quickly with 2 wooden spoons to coat carrots with a thin film of oil.
3. Add broth and oyster sauce, and cook over high heat 10 minutes. The liquid should be reduced almost to a glaze. Stir carrots from time to time to be sure they are evenly glazed. Remove from heat and turn into serving bowl.

Karen Lee

Karen Lee, a New York-based author and cooking teacher, describes Chinese cooking as "physically demanding—an action cuisine," which is actually both relaxing and fascinating when you know how to approach it. She emphasizes the importance of proper equipment—a sharp knife or cleaver and a good pan—because these make the work go quickly and produce the best results. For a successful stir fry, she prefers a flat-bottomed wok or heavy skillet. Remember that the essence of stir frying is speed, so prepare and organize all ingredients in the correct cooking order. Reheat oil between batches and quickly add the ingredients. The food cooks almost at once if the heat is high enough and if you do not overcrowd the pan.

Karen Lee was once the assistant of Grace Zia Chu, a famous Chinese cook, but she has developed her own cooking methods, which stress using little fat or salt. Her recipes are her own versions of Chinese classics and are based on homemade stocks and sauces and the freshest ingredients.

The three menus represent a mélange of Chinese regional fare, with contrasting tastes and colors. In Menu 1, the smoky taste of the bean sprouts offsets the fiery chili shrimp. The orange chicken in Menu 2 is spicy, aromatic, and sweet. Menu 3 features a northern Chinese favorite, barbecued lamb, served with braised turnips, which Eastern Chinese believe to have a medicinal effect, and Szechwan-style string beans flavored with dried shrimp and preserved vegetables.

This meal of shrimp, diced chicken, and bean sprouts comes to the table on serving dishes decorated with a delicate Chinese motif. Set off the shrimp by turning them out on a bed of lettuce leaves. Chopsticks and straw place mats will add attractive Oriental accents to this simple but authentic menu.

Chili Shrimp
Smoked Bean Sprouts
Diced Chicken with Fermented Black Beans / Rice

This chili shrimp dish is typical of Szechwan. Chinese chilies range from the firebrands used in sauces and oils to the larger, milder ones. Chinese cooks often use chilies stirred into a paste with garlic, as in this recipe.

The Chinese frequently cook shrimp with the shells still on, actually scorching the shells to intensify the shrimp flavor. This method has another benefit—it cuts down preparation time.

The smoked bean sprouts and diced chicken breasts are Cantonese. The fermented black beans in the chicken recipe are very pungent, so before using them you may wish to rinse them to remove some of the saltiness.

When buying bean sprouts, avoid the kind that are sold soaking in water. They will not scorch and thus will not take on the proper smoky flavor.

WHAT TO DRINK

Here you need a full-bodied, dry wine: a white Burgundy from Mâcon or an inexpensive California Chardonnay.

SHOPPING LIST AND STAPLES

1 pound skinless, boneless chicken breasts
16 large shrimp (about 1 pound)
1 bunch scallions
½ pound shallots (about 10 whole)
1 leek
¾ pound mung bean sprouts (not soaked in water)
4 Chinese dried black mushrooms
8-ounce package fermented black beans
Fresh ginger
2 cloves garlic
1 egg
2 tablespoons Chinese Chicken Stock (see page 13)
1 tablespoon oyster sauce
3 cups plus 4 tablespoons plus 2 teaspoons peanut oil
1 teaspoon Oriental sesame oil
2 tablespoons plus 1½ teaspoons dark soy sauce
3 teaspoons light soy sauce
1 teaspoon Chinese red rice vinegar or Western red wine vinegar
1 teaspoon chili paste
1 cup uncooked rice
2 tablespoons water chestnut powder, preferably, or cornstarch
1 tablespoon plus ½ teaspoon sugar
7 tablespoons dry sherry

UTENSILS

Wok
　　or Dutch oven (for chicken)
　　and 12-inch skillet (for shrimp; bean sprouts)
Medium-size saucepan with cover (for rice)
Large bowl
Medium-size bowl
4 small bowls
Metal colander
Strainer
Measuring cups and spoons
Chinese cleaver or chef's knife
Paring knife
Metal wok spatula
16-inch chopsticks or 2 long-handled wooden spoons
Deep-fat thermometer
Small scissors, preferably embroidery-type

START-TO-FINISH STEPS

1. Follow general rice recipe on page 12, step 1. Bring 1 cup water to a boil and follow bean sprouts recipe step 1.
2. Follow general rice recipe step 2.
3. Combine marinade ingredients in chicken recipe step 1 and follow steps 2 and 3. Preheat oven to 200 degrees.
4. Follow bean sprouts recipe steps 2 and 3.
5. Follow shrimp recipe steps 1 and 2.
6. Remove saucepan from heat in rice recipe step 3.
7. Follow bean sprouts recipe steps 4 through 6.
8. Follow chicken recipe steps 4 and 5.
9. Complete bean sprouts recipe steps 7 through 9 and keep warm in preheated oven, if desired.
10. Wipe out wok. Complete chicken, steps 6 through 11.
11. Wipe out wok (or skillet used for bean sprouts). Follow shrimp recipe steps 3 through 6; follow general rice recipe step 4.
12. Remove bean sprouts and chicken from oven. Serve together with shrimp and rice on the side.

RECIPES

Chili Shrimp

The seasoning sauce:
2 tablespoons dry sherry
1 tablespoon sugar
1 teaspoon Chinese red rice vinegar or Western red wine vinegar

1 tablespoon dark soy sauce
1½ teaspoons light soy sauce
2 tablespoons Chinese Chicken Stock
1 teaspoon chili paste
1 teaspoon water chestnut powder or cornstarch

16 large shrimp (about 1 pound)
2 whole scallions, chopped
2 teaspoons minced fresh ginger
1 clove garlic, minced
2½ tablespoons plus 2 teaspoons peanut oil
1 teaspoon sesame oil

1. Combine seasoning sauce ingredients in small bowl. Stir to dissolve water chestnut powder or cornstarch.
2. Using small pair of scissors, cut shell along back of shrimp, cutting into shrimp about halfway through. Do not remove shell. Remove dark vein with nose of scissors and pull off legs. Rinse shrimp under cold running water, drain in colander, and pat dry.
3. Heat wok or heavy skillet over high heat about 1 minute. Add 2½ tablespoons peanut oil and heat until hot but not smoking. Add shrimp and stir fry about 5 minutes, or until shrimp are almost cooked through. Shrimp will be charred and deep orange in color. Empty shrimp onto warm serving platter.
4. Return pan to high heat and add remaining 2 teaspoons peanut oil. Stir fry scallions, ginger, and garlic 30 seconds.
5. Stir seasoning sauce once more and add it all at once to wok or skillet, stirring until sauce thickens slightly.
6. Return shrimp to pan and stir another minute, or until shrimp are evenly coated with sauce. Turn off heat and swirl in sesame oil. Empty contents onto serving platter.

Smoked Bean Sprouts

4 Chinese dried black mushrooms
1 medium-size leek, white part only
¾ pound mung bean sprouts
1 teaspoon water chestnut powder or cornstarch
1 tablespoon oyster sauce
1½ teaspoons dark soy sauce
1 tablespoon dry sherry
1½ tablespoons peanut oil

1. Cover mushrooms with 1 cup boiling water and allow to soak 20 to 30 minutes.
2. Cut off root end of leek. Slice leek in half lengthwise and rinse under warm water to remove all sand. Cut into 3-inch lengths; then shred. Set aside in small bowl.
3. Place sprouts on layers of paper towels and pat dry.
4. Squeeze each mushroom over bowl. Using strainer lined with double thickness of cheesecloth or paper towels, strain and reserve 1 tablespoon of the liquid. Remove tough stems, rinse under cold water to get rid of any grit trapped in gills, and shred mushrooms. Add to leeks.
5. Combine water chestnut powder or cornstarch, oyster sauce, soy sauce, and sherry with the tablespoon of mushroom soaking liquid. Stir to dissolve.
6. Heat wok or skillet over high heat 2 minutes. Add bean

sprouts, reserving a sprinkling for garnish, if desired. Stir fry without oil 2 or 3 minutes, or until sprouts begin to scorch. Transfer cooked sprouts to flat serving dish.
7. Return wok or skillet to high heat and add peanut oil. Immediately add mushrooms and leeks, and stir fry 2 minutes.
8. Stir oyster sauce mixture once more and add to the vegetables all at once, stirring until sauce thickens.
9. Add the cooked bean sprouts and mix briefly. Empty contents onto serving dish. This dish may be eaten hot or served at room temperature, garnished with a sprinkling of some fresh sprouts, if desired.

Diced Chicken with Fermented Black Beans

1 egg white
1 tablespoon water chestnut powder or cornstarch
1 tablespoon dry sherry
1 pound skinless, boneless chicken breasts

The seasoning sauce:
3 tablespoons dry sherry
1 tablespoon dark soy sauce
1½ teaspoons light soy sauce
½ teaspoon sugar
1 teaspoon water chestnut powder or cornstarch

¾ cup shallots (about 10 whole)
2 teaspoons minced fresh ginger
1 clove garlic, minced
1½ tablespoons fermented black beans
3 cups peanut oil

1. Combine egg white, water chestnut powder or cornstarch, and dry sherry in medium-size bowl and stir vigorously about 1 minute, or until marinade is smooth.
2. Remove any cartilage and fat from chicken. Cut into ¾-inch pieces and add to marinade, tossing well until chicken is evenly coated.
3. Combine seasoning sauce ingredients in small bowl. Stir to dissolve water chestnut powder or cornstarch.
4. Peel shallots and leave them whole.
5. Combine ginger, garlic, and black beans in small bowl.
6. Heat wok or Dutch oven over high heat about 1 minute. Pour in peanut oil and heat until oil reaches 350 degrees or until a sliver of garlic sizzles on contact.
7. Stir chicken in marinade. Turn heat to high and add mixture to pan all at once, stirring in circular motion about 1½ minutes, or until chicken turns opaque.
8. Turn off heat and carefully drain chicken and hot oil in metal colander set over large bowl.
9. Return 1 tablespoon of the oil to the wok or to a heavy skillet and add shallots. Stir occasionally over low heat about 3 minutes, or until shallots are cooked through.
10. Turn heat to high and add ginger, garlic, and black beans. Stir another minute.
11. Stir seasoning sauce and add it to the pan along with the cooked chicken. Stir another minute, or until chicken is evenly coated. Empty pan onto heated serving dish and keep warm in oven.

Orange Chicken
Stir-Fried Snow Peas
Stir-Fried Spinach with Fermented Bean Curd

Red peppers, scallion tops, and orange peel create an appetizing mélange of color with browned chicken thighs. The peas and stir-fried spinach add two more contrasting greens. Garnish the meal with semicircles of orange.

The crisp chicken dish in this menu is an excellent example of Szechwan cooking, successfully combining the sting of chilies in the chili paste with the mild aftertaste of the slightly sweet seasoning sauce. Orange peel, a favorite Szechwan flavoring, is also an ingredient. If you cannot find dried Chinese orange or tangerine peel, substitute fresh grated peel. Just be sure to grate the peel only; do not include any of the bitter white pith.

Snow peas are likely to scorch, so stir fry them quickly over medium heat. Sugar snap peas work equally well, and unlike other Western peas, they do not need to be shelled before cooking. For a few days' storage, wrap unwashed peas in a plastic bag and refrigerate.

Both the chicken and the spinach recipes call for water chestnut powder as a thickening agent. Cornstarch is less expensive and perfectly adequate—and also more readily available—but use the chestnut powder if possible; it is lighter and gives a more luminous cast to foods. To remove any lumpiness, pulverize the powder in a blender and store it in an airtight jar. You will find water chestnut powder in Chinese groceries.

The fermented bean curd in the stir-fried spinach recipe has a strong, cheesy taste when mashed. Available in Chinese groceries as bottled cubes, it keeps indefinitely in the refrigerator. Several brands are seasoned with chili flakes. Buy one of these if you like extra spice. There are no Western equivalents. If you cannot find fermented bean curd, simply omit bean curd from the recipe; plain bean curd is not a substitute.

WHAT TO DRINK

Here, a medley of delicate flavors calls for an equally delicate wine with a light touch of sweetness. A German wine—say a Riesling Kabinett or, possibly, an Auslese (which is slightly sweeter than Kabinett) should be your first choice. Look for one from the Rheingau or the Rheinhessen.

SHOPPING LIST AND STAPLES

2 pounds chicken thighs
1½ pounds fresh spinach
¾ pound fresh snow peas or sugar snap peas
1 medium-size red bell pepper
1 orange (optional)
1 bunch scallions
Fresh ginger
3 cloves garlic
1 egg
2 tablespoons Chinese Chicken Stock (see page 13)
1 small jar fermented bean curd (optional)
3 cups plus 3 tablespoons peanut oil
3 teaspoons Oriental sesame oil
1 tablespoon dark soy sauce
1 tablespoon light soy sauce
1 teaspoon Chinese red rice vinegar
Dash white distilled vinegar

1 teaspoon chili paste
1 tablespoon plus 3 teaspoons water chestnut powder, preferably, or cornstarch
2 tablespoons plus 1 teaspoon sugar
Salt
1 ounce Chinese dried orange or tangerine peel, or 1 teaspoon grated fresh peel
5 tablespoons dry sherry

UTENSILS

Wok
    or Dutch oven (for chicken)
    and 12-inch skillet (for completing chicken; snow peas; spinach)
9-by-12-inch baking sheet
Large mixing bowl
3 small bowls
Salad spinner (optional)
Measuring cups and spoons
Chinese cleaver or chef's knife
Paring knife
Metal wok spatula
Chinese mesh spoon or long-handled slotted metal spoon
16-inch chopsticks or 2 long-handled wooden spoons
Deep-fat thermometer

START-TO-FINISH STEPS

1. Follow chicken recipe steps 1 and 2.
2. Follow spinach recipe steps 1 and 2, and snow peas recipe step 1.
3. Grate fresh orange or tangerine peel, if using, and follow chicken recipe steps 3 through 6.
4. Slice scallions in spinach recipe, step 3.
5. Complete chicken recipe, steps 7 through 16.
6. Wipe out wok. Complete spinach recipe steps 4 through 6. If you desire warm spinach, keep in oven with chicken while you finish preparing snow peas.
7. Wipe out wok or skillet for spinach. Follow snow peas recipe steps 2 and 3. Serve platter of chicken with snow peas and pass the spinach separately.

RECIPES

Orange Chicken

The chicken and marinade:
2 pounds chicken thighs
1 egg white
1 tablespoon plus 2 teaspoons water chestnut powder or cornstarch
1 tablespoon dry sherry

The seasoning sauce:
1 teaspoon water chestnut powder or cornstarch
3 tablespoons dry sherry
1 tablespoon dark soy sauce
1 tablespoon light soy sauce
2 tablespoons Chinese Chicken Stock

2 tablespoons sugar
1 teaspoon chili paste
1 teaspoon Chinese red rice vinegar

1 medium-size red bell pepper
3 whole scallions
2 teaspoons minced fresh ginger
2 cloves garlic, minced
3 pieces Chinese dried orange or tangerine peel, approximately 1½ by 2 inches, or 1 teaspoon grated fresh peel
3 cups peanut oil
2 teaspoons sesame oil
1 orange, halved and sliced for garnish (optional)

1. Remove skin from chicken thighs and cut away any fat. Using heavy cleaver or chef's knife, cut chicken thighs crosswise through bone into 1½-inch pieces.
2. Combine marinade ingredients in large bowl and add chicken pieces. Stir vigorously about 1 minute, until marinade is smooth and chicken is evenly coated. Cover and refrigerate until ready to cook.
3. Combine seasoning sauce ingredients in small bowl. Stir to dissolve water chestnut powder or cornstarch.
4. Core and seed red pepper and split in half. Slice into ¾-inch squares. Cut each square into 2 triangles.
5. Firmly grasp scallions together and slice them into ¼-inch rounds. Break orange peel into ¼-inch pieces.
6. Heat wok or Dutch oven over high heat about 1 minute. Pour in 3 cups peanut oil and turn heat to medium. Heat oil until it reaches 350 degrees on deep-fat thermometer.
7. Stir chicken once more in marinade. Raise heat to high and add half the chicken pieces and marinade to the oil, stirring occasionally to prevent chicken pieces from sticking together. Cook about 3 to 5 minutes, or until chicken is lightly browned.
8. Using Chinese mesh spoon or long-handled slotted metal spoon, remove chicken pieces from oil and place them on baking sheet lined with several layers of paper towels. Before frying remaining chicken, bring oil back to 350 degrees.
9. To finish cooking chicken (this gives it a crispy crust), heat oil to 375 degrees. Return one fourth of the chicken to the oil and fry 1 minute, or until chicken is well browned. Drain on fresh paper towels and fry remaining chicken in batches.
10. If using wok, pour off all but 1 tablespoon of the hot oil. Otherwise, heat heavy skillet 1 minute and add the tablespoon of hot oil.
11. Preheat oven to 200 degrees.
12. Turn heat to low, add scallions, ginger, and garlic, and stir fry 15 seconds.
13. Add dried or fresh grated peel and stir fry until it turns a darker brown, about 1 minute.
14. Raise heat to high, add red pepper, and stir fry 30 seconds.
15. Stir seasoning sauce and add it to pan all at once, stirring until sauce thickens slightly, about 15 seconds.
16. Return cooked chicken to pan all at once and stir fry

rapidly until chicken has been evenly glazed with the sauce. Turn off heat and add sesame oil, stirring to blend. Empty contents onto heated flat serving dish and keep warm in oven.

Note: If desired, oil may be heated to 375 degrees in step 6 and chicken fried 5 to 6 minutes, or until crisp and golden brown. This would eliminate the second frying process in step 9.

Stir-Fried Snow Peas

¾ pound snow peas or sugar snap peas
2 tablespoons peanut oil
½ teaspoon salt
½ teaspoon sugar

1. String peas and rinse under cold running water. Drain and dry well with paper towels or in salad spinner.
2. Heat wok or skillet over high heat about 1 minute. Add peanut oil and heat until hot but not smoking. Lower heat to medium and add salt and sugar, stirring a few seconds.
3. Add snow peas or sugar snaps and stir fry continuously 1 minute. Remove peas and arrange them around chicken on serving platter like spokes of a wheel, if you wish.

Stir-Fried Spinach with Fermented Bean Curd

The seasoning sauce:
1 teaspoon water chestnut powder or cornstarch
1 tablespoon dry sherry
1 small square fermented bean curd, mashed (optional)
½ teaspoon sugar

1½ pounds fresh spinach
Dash white distilled vinegar
1 clove garlic, minced
2 whole scallions
½ teaspoon salt
1 tablespoon peanut oil
1 teaspoon sesame oil

1. Combine seasoning sauce ingredients in small bowl. Stir to dissolve water chestnut powder or cornstarch.
2. Remove stems from spinach and wash in several changes of cold water to which a dash of white vinegar has been added—it helps rid spinach of any grit. Dry with paper towels or in salad spinner.
3. Firmly grasp scallions together and slice them into ½-inch rounds.
4. Heat wok or heavy skillet over high heat about 1 minute. Add peanut oil and heat until it is hot but not smoking. If a piece of scallion sizzles when added, oil is hot enough. Add salt and stir until it dissolves. Add garlic and scallions, and stir fry 30 seconds.
5. Add spinach and stir fry about 2 minutes, or until leaves wilt.
6. Stir seasoning sauce and add it to pan all at once, stirring until spinach is evenly coated with sauce. Turn off heat and add sesame oil, stirring to mix. Empty contents onto serving dish. The spinach may be served warm or at room temperature.

Barbecued Lamb
Sautéed String Beans, Szechwan Style
Braised Turnips with Black Mushrooms

Precision-cut turnips and trimmed string beans add visual appeal to this menu of barbecued lamb cubes. Muted in color, *the meal benefits from a sprinkling of sliced scallion greens, which complement the green beans.*

The barbecued lamb marinated in black tea and fragrant with garlic and hot chili oil is a northern Chinese dish that is particularly good grilled on an outdoor barbecue in summer. Various cuts of beef, such as sirloin, flank, or shell steak, or filet mignon, make good substitutes for lamb. Instead of a Chinese sesame paste for the lamb's marinade, Karen Lee uses tahini, a Middle Eastern condiment, whose flavor she prefers for this recipe.

String beans that are deep fried and then quickly stir fried are a famous Szechwan dish. Despite their double cooking, the beans retain their natural crispness. The cooks of this far western region often add ground pork to the beans for extra protein and flavor. In this version dried shrimp and Tientsin preserved vegetable also flavor the beans. The tiny dried shrimp have a salty taste and a strong odor, and are valued as a highly seasoned condiment. There is no comparable Western substitute. The preserved vegetable is shredded cabbage, which adds a distinctive crunch and saltiness to the recipe. It is sold in bulk in plastic bags, or in ceramic crocks in Chinese provision stores.

The turnips are easy to do. You steam them briefly, then stir fry, and finally braise them in a rich liquid. You can make them ahead if you wish and quickly reheat them, taking care not to overcook them. Their soft texture is an interesting contrast to the crunchy beans.

WHAT TO DRINK

The interplay of sweet and spicy in this meal makes choosing a wine a challenge. You might serve beer or, even better, a good ale. For a wine, try a French Colombard from California or perhaps a California or Washington State Semillon. Their softness will accommodate the variety of tastes in the menu.

SHOPPING LIST AND STAPLES

1½ pounds boneless leg of lamb
¼ pound ground pork
1 pound small white turnips
1 pound string beans
1 bunch scallions
5 to 6 Chinese dried black mushrooms
Fresh ginger
2 cloves garlic
15-ounce can tahini (Middle Eastern sesame seed paste)
12-ounce can Tientsin preserved vegetable
3 cups plus 1½ tablespoons peanut oil
1½ tablespoons Oriental sesame oil
1 tablespoon hot chili oil
5 tablespoons dark soy sauce
1½ tablespoons Western red wine vinegar
1 teaspoon chili paste
1 teaspoon honey
4-ounce bag dried shrimp
2½ tablespoons sugar

Chinese black tea
2 tablespoons dry sherry

UTENSILS

Wok
    or Dutch oven (for string beans)
    and 12-inch skillet (for completing string beans; turnips)
Large saucepan with cover
Vegetable steamer
2 large mixing bowls
3 small bowls
Metal colander
Strainer
Measuring cups and spoons
Chinese cleaver or chef's knife
Paring knife
Metal wok spatula
Chinese mesh spoon or long-handled slotted metal spoon
16-inch chopsticks or 2 long-handled wooden spoons
Deep-fat thermometer
8 skewers, preferably bamboo

START-TO-FINISH STEPS

In the morning: Bring ¾ cup water to a boil and follow lamb recipe steps 1 through 4.
1. Bring 2 cups water to a boil. Use 1 cup for shrimp in string beans recipe step 1 and the other for mushrooms in turnips recipe step 1.
2. Remove lamb from refrigerator and bring to room temperature, step 5. If using bamboo skewers, soak in water to prevent scorching.
3. Follow turnip recipe steps 2 and 3.
4. Follow lamb recipe step 6.
5. Follow string beans recipe steps 2 and 3.
6. Follow lamb recipe step 7 and turnip recipe steps 4 and 5.
7. If using double oven, preheat oven to 200 degrees. If using single-oven range, turn off heat. Follow lamb recipe step 8.
8. Complete turnip recipe steps 6 and 7, and keep warm in oven.
9. Wipe out wok. Follow string beans recipe steps 4 through 9.
10. Remove barbecued lamb and cooked turnips and mushrooms from oven. Serve with string beans.

RECIPES

Barbecued Lamb

1 tablespoon black tea leaves
½ cup tahini (sesame seed paste)
3 tablespoons dark soy sauce
1½ tablespoons sesame oil
1 tablespoon hot chili oil
1½ tablespoons sugar
1½ tablespoons Western red wine vinegar

2 whole scallions, chopped
2 cloves garlic, minced
1½ pounds boneless leg of lamb

1. Pour ¾ cup boiling water over tea leaves in large bowl and steep 5 minutes. Strain tea into measuring cup to make ½ cup. Discard leaves.
2. Return tea to large bowl and combine with remaining ingredients except lamb, and stir to mix well.
3. Using Chinese cleaver or chef's knife, cut lamb into 1¼-inch cubes.
4. Add lamb to marinade. Turn lamb to coat well and seal tightly. Refrigerate.
5. Thirty minutes before cooking, remove lamb from refrigerator.
6. Preheat broiler.
7. Place 4 or 5 cubes of lamb on each skewer, leaving ½ inch between cubes. Place skewers an inch apart on broiler rack and set rack as close as possible to heat source.
8. Broil 8 to 10 minutes, turning frequently. Keep warm in oven.

Sautéed String Beans, Szechwan Style

1 teaspoon dried shrimp
1 pound string beans
1 tablespoon dark soy sauce
1 tablespoon dry sherry
1 teaspoon chili paste
1 teaspoon honey
3 cups peanut oil
¼ pound ground pork
2 teaspoons minced fresh ginger
1 tablespoon Tientsin preserved vegetable
1 whole scallion, chopped

1. In small bowl, cover shrimp with boiling water and allow to soak 20 minutes. Drain and mince.
2. Cut off stem ends of string beans, leaving pointed ends intact. Wash beans and dry them well so they will not spatter when frying.
3. Combine soy sauce, sherry, chili paste, and honey in small bowl.
4. Heat wok or Dutch oven over high heat about 1 minute. Pour in oil and heat over medium heat until oil reaches 375 degrees on deep-fat thermometer. Or, test oil with a string bean: it should sizzle and the oil foam around it.
5. Turn heat to high and carefully add string beans all at once. Deep fry them until they wrinkle, about 3 minutes. Drain beans and hot oil in colander set over large bowl. Alternatively, you may use a Chinese mesh spoon or long-handled slotted metal spoon and quickly scoop out beans and drain them in a metal colander.
6. Return 1 tablespoon of the hot peanut oil to the wok or to a heavy skillet and turn heat to high. Add ground pork and stir about 2 minutes, or until pork turns white.
7. Add shrimp, ginger, preserved vegetable, and scallion. Cook, stirring, another minute.

8. Stir soy sauce mixture to recombine ingredients and add it to pan all at once, stirring a few seconds.
9. Add cooked, drained string beans and stir fry another minute, or until sauce is completely absorbed. Empty contents of pan onto heated flat serving dish and serve immediately.

Braised Turnips with Black Mushrooms

5 to 6 Chinese dried black mushrooms
1 pound small white turnips
1 tablespoon sugar
1 tablespoon dark soy sauce
1 tablespoon dry sherry
1½ tablespoons peanut oil

1. Cover mushrooms with 1 cup boiling water and allow to soak 20 to 30 minutes.
2. Peel turnips and cut into 1-inch cubes.
3. Bring 1 inch of water to a boil in large saucepan fitted with a vegetable steamer. Steam turnips 10 minutes.
4. Squeeze each mushroom over small bowl in which mushrooms soaked. Strain and reserve ½ cup of the liquid. Remove tough stems and rinse mushrooms under cold running water to rid of any grit trapped in gills. Cut each mushroom into quarters or eighths, depending on its size.
5. Add sugar, soy sauce, and sherry to bowl with reserved mushroom liquid.
6. Heat wok or heavy skillet over high heat about 1 minute. Add peanut oil and heat until hot but not smoking. Add mushrooms and turnips, and stir fry about 1 minute.
7. Stir soy sauce mixture before adding it to pan. Stir until turnips and mushrooms are evenly glazed. Turn into heated serving dish.

LEFTOVER SUGGESTION

The marinade for the lamb also makes a very good dip for lightly blanched or raw vegetables. The barbecued lamb is particularly good served the next day. Bring it to room temperature. Do not reheat it; the meat will dry out. The leftover green beans, if any, combined with greens, make an excellent salad.

ADDED TOUCH

Ripe, seasonal fresh fruit, served with scented or semi-fermented tea, brings any Chinese meal to a satisfying close. Pineapple and strawberries, when they are in the market, are a good combination. Slice off the top and bottom of a fresh pineapple, and save the top. Cut the body into 6 sections lengthwise. Remove the hard inner core and separate the fruit from the rind with your knife. Then cut each piece into 6 sections vertically. Place the top of the pineapple in the center of a serving platter and arrange the 6 sections around it, so that they radiate outward like wheel spokes. Scatter whole strawberries around the spokes and sprinkle with ¼ cup Grand Marnier.

Mai Leung

MENU 1 (Left)
Spinach and Egg Shred Soup
Diced Chicken, Szechwan Style
Stir-Fried Green Beans with Garlic
Rice

MENU 2
Five-Fragrance Oyster Fritters
Steamed Sesame Eggplant
Jade-Green Broccoli

MENU 3
Pork Shreds and Szechwan Pickle Soup
Beef and Scallops with Oyster Sauce
Stir-Fried Snow Peas with
Mushrooms and Almonds
Rice

C ooking teacher and author Mai Leung is another cook who believes that Chinese cuisine is
effortless—once you learn the basic methods.
She advises her beginning students to follow
recipes carefully until they gain confidence but then to
experiment with ingredients and seasonings. She also
stresses the importance of understanding the differences
in spices and sauces. For instance, there are several kinds
of soy sauce and oyster sauce, varying in aroma and flavor.
As you use them, you will learn to recognize the most
subtle distinctions and to know when to use one rather
than another in a particular recipe.

When she was living in Hong Kong, Mai Leung learned
to cook in the southern style of that area. She studied with
chefs from other regions as well and gained even more
knowledge of other regional approaches during her travels
throughout China.

In Canton and Hong Kong, southern coastal regions
that are famous for their abundant fresh oysters, resi-
dents rarely eat oysters raw, but they have created innu-
merable oyster-based recipes. Oyster fritters are featured
in Menu 2, and oyster sauce (made from ground oysters)
flavors the beef and scallop dish in Menu 3.

*Oriental dinnerware and bamboo place mats set off the bril-
liant colors of this Szechwan meal of diced chicken and stir-
fried green beans. A glass soup bowl shows off the clarity of the
broth, which is filled with crisp spinach and slivers of white
bean curd.*

95

Spinach and Egg Shred Soup
Diced Chicken, Szechwan Style
Stir-Fried Green Beans with Garlic / Rice

This spicy meal of diced chicken, garlicky stir-fried green beans, and a clear broth contains no ingredients unfamiliar to Westerners. The soup is a typical Chinese broth embellished with crisp vegetables and slivers of meat, meant to be refreshing rather than filling. You may serve the soup as the Chinese traditionally do, as part of the meal.

The Szechwan-style stir-fried chicken dish is made zesty by the use of dried red chilies. Serving stir-fried green beans with cooked ground pork, as in this recipe, is a typical Szechwan way of combining tastes and textures.

WHAT TO DRINK

This Szechwan-style menu, with its marked presence of hot peppers and garlic, will go well with a lightly sweet wine: try a German Riesling from the Rheingau.

SHOPPING LIST AND STAPLES

1 pound skinless, boneless chicken breasts (about 2 whole breasts)
2 ounces ground pork
1 pound young green beans
¼ pound fresh spinach
1 small red bell pepper
1 bunch scallions
Fresh ginger
3 medium-size cloves garlic
2 eggs
8-ounce can water chestnuts
4 cups Chinese Chicken Stock (see page 13)
2 cups plus 3 tablespoons peanut or corn oil
2½ teaspoons Oriental sesame oil
2 tablespoons dark soy sauce
1½ tablespoons catsup
1 tablespoon white vinegar
1 cup uncooked rice
1 tablespoon plus 2 teaspoons cornstarch
2 tablespoons plus ¾ teaspoon sugar
Salt
2 dried red chili peppers
⅛ teaspoon Cayenne pepper
1 tablespoon dried cloud ear mushrooms
¼ cup raw unsalted peanuts, shelled and hulled
3 tablespoons Chinese rice wine or dry sherry

UTENSILS

Wok
  or Dutch oven (for cooking chicken)
  and 12-inch skillet (for completing chicken; green beans)
Small skillet
2 large saucepans, 1 with cover
Medium-size saucepan with cover (for rice)
2 trays or plates
Large mixing bowl
4 small bowls
Metal colander
Measuring cups and spoons
Chinese cleaver or chef's knife
Paring knife
Chinese mesh spoon or long-handled slotted metal spoon
16-inch chopsticks or 2 long-handled wooden spoons
Meat pounder (optional)

START-TO-FINISH STEPS

1. Follow diced chicken recipe step 1.
2. Follow spinach soup recipe step 1.
3. Follow general rice recipe on page 12, steps 1 and 2.
4. Peel and mince ginger; slice scallions; rinse and quarter water chestnuts; seed, trim, and chop red bell pepper. Follow chicken recipe steps 2 through 4.
5. Follow spinach soup recipe steps 2 through 4.
6. Follow general rice recipe step 3.
7. Follow diced chicken recipe steps 5 through 8.
8. Preheat oven to 200 degrees. Follow stir-fried green beans recipe steps 1 through 4.
9. Complete diced chicken recipe, steps 9 through 12.
10. Wipe out pan. Follow stir-fried green beans recipe steps 5 through 7.
11. Follow spinach soup recipe step 5 and general rice recipe step 4. Serve.

RECIPES

Spinach and Egg Shred Soup

¼ pound fresh spinach
4 cups Chinese Chicken Stock
1 egg, lightly beaten with ¼ teaspoon salt
¼ teaspoon salt plus to taste
1 tablespoon peanut or corn oil

¼ teaspoon sugar
½ teaspoon sesame oil

1. Wash spinach well, rinsing to remove any grit or sand. Snap off any tough stems. Drain in colander.
2. Bring chicken stock to a boil in large saucepan. Reduce to a simmer and cover.
3. Heat small skillet over moderate heat and add cooking oil, turning pan to film bottom. When oil is hot, swirl in egg mixture to make large thin pancake. When egg is set—it will take only a minute—flip egg and turn off heat.
4. Transfer "pancake" to chopping board and cut into thin strips. Set aside.
5. Turn spinach into the simmering stock and turn off heat. Stir in sugar, sesame oil, and egg strips. Add salt to taste. Serve hot.

Diced Chicken, Szechwan Style

1 tablespoon dried cloud ear mushrooms
1 pound skinless, boneless chicken breasts (about 2 whole breasts)
1 egg white
1 tablespoon plus 2 teaspoons cornstarch
2 tablespoons sugar
1 tablespoon dark soy sauce
1 tablespoon white vinegar
2 tablespoons Chinese rice wine or dry sherry
1½ tablespoons catsup
1 tablespoon water
⅛ teaspoon Cayenne pepper
¼ teaspoon salt
2 teaspoons sesame oil
2 dried red chili peppers
2 quarter-size slices fresh ginger, peeled and minced
3 scallions, cut into thin rounds
6 water chestnuts, thoroughly rinsed and quartered
½ small red bell pepper, seeds and ribs removed, cut into ½-inch squares
2 cups peanut or corn oil
¼ cup raw unsalted peanuts, shelled and hulled

1. Cover dried cloud ears with 1 cup hot water and allow to soak 20 minutes, or until they are soft and triple in size.
2. Pound chicken breasts gently with flat side of cleaver or with meat pounder. Trim any fat and cut into ½-inch cubes. Put lightly beaten egg white in large mixing bowl and slowly stir in 1 tablespoon cornstarch, to combine well. Add cubed chicken and toss well. Set aside.
3. Combine sugar, remaining cornstarch, soy sauce, vinegar, wine, catsup, water, Cayenne pepper, salt, and sesame oil in small bowl.
4. Group chili peppers, minced ginger, scallions, water chestnuts, and red bell pepper on tray or large plate.
5. Drain and tear each cloud ear into 4 or 5 pieces. Set aside.
6. Heat wok or Dutch oven over high heat until a bead of water evaporates on contact. Add cooking oil and heat until very hot but not smoking—a good test is to see whether a small piece of scallion sizzles when dropped in the oil. Add peanuts and turn heat to medium-low. Deep fry peanuts until golden brown, about 3 to 5 minutes. Remove with Chinese mesh spoon or long-handled slotted metal spoon and put on paper towels to drain.
7. Add chicken mixture to the hot oil and turn off heat. Separate chicken pieces with cooking chopsticks or 2 wooden spoons. As soon as chicken pieces turn white, use Chinese mesh spoon or slotted metal spoon to remove them to a plate lined with paper towels and set aside.
8. If you used a wok, pour off all but 2 tablespoons of warm cooking oil into a container; if you used a Dutch oven, pour off all the oil into a container and store. (Strain and save cooking oil for other Chinese dishes.)
9. Return wok to high heat or use a large, deep skillet to which you have added 2 tablespoons of warm cooking oil. When oil is very hot, add chili peppers, which are used to flavor the oil, and cook until they turn dark red. Remove and discard.
10. Add ginger, half the scallions, the cloud ears, water chestnuts, and red bell pepper. Stir fry 3 or 4 seconds.
11. Stir soy sauce mixture, swirl it into the vegetables, and cook, stirring, until sauce begins to bubble. Return chicken to pan and cook, stirring constantly, several seconds to reheat. Transfer to serving platter and top with peanuts and remaining scallions.
12. Keep warm in preheated 200-degree oven while preparing other dishes.

Stir-Fried Green Beans with Garlic

1 pound fresh young green beans, washed and trimmed
¼ teaspoon salt
½ teaspoon sugar
1 tablespoon dark soy sauce
1 tablespoon Chinese rice wine or dry sherry
2 tablespoons water
2 scallions
3 medium-size cloves garlic, minced
2 tablespoons peanut or corn oil
2 ounces ground pork

1. Bring 2 quarts water to a boil in large saucepan.
2. Add green beans and blanch about 45 seconds over moderate heat, then pour into colander and rinse under cold running water to stop the cooking. Drain.
3. Combine salt, sugar, soy sauce, wine, and water in small bowl.
4. Wash and trim scallions, leaving some of green tips, and slice them in half lengthwise. Cut into 1½-inch pieces.
5. Heat wok or heavy skillet over high heat until a bead of water evaporates on contact and add oil. When oil is hot, add scallions and garlic, and stir fry 4 or 5 seconds. Add ground pork and stir fry continuously until it loses its pink color, about 1 to 2 minutes.
6. Stir soy sauce mixture and swirl into wok. Add green beans and stir over moderate heat about 1 minute, or just until they are heated through.
7. Cover and keep warm until ready to serve.

Five-Fragrance Oyster Fritters
Steamed Sesame Eggplant
Jade-Green Broccoli

This light meal of oyster fritters, eggplant, and broccoli is served attractively on an interestingly shaped dinner plate nested in a bamboo tray. Accompany the fritters with a bowl of the dipping sauce.

Crisp vegetables set off this light meal, where the emphasis is on steaming and blanching rather than on stir frying. Both broccoli and eggplant must be very fresh.

Cantonese chefs have created numerous delicious oyster-based recipes. These fritters, seasoned with Chinese five-spice, white pepper, and sliced scallions, are served with a ginger-soy-vinegar dipping sauce.

WHAT TO DRINK

The oysters need a crisp, lightly sweet wine, such as a California Semillon or Chenin Blanc.

SHOPPING LIST AND STAPLES

16 to 18 large fresh oysters, shucked, or 2 eight-ounce containers shucked oysters, drained
1 small bunch broccoli
1 eggplant (about 1 pound)
1 head Boston or Bibb lettuce (optional)
1 large bunch scallions
Fresh ginger
4 eggs
3 tablespoons *hoisin* sauce
2 tablespoons oyster sauce
½ cup plus 8 tablespoons peanut or corn oil
2 teaspoons Oriental sesame oil
4 tablespoons dark soy sauce
¼ cup Chinese red rice vinegar
⅔ cup all-purpose flour
1½ teaspoons baking powder
1½ teaspoons Chinese five-spice
Salt
¼ teaspoon freshly ground white pepper
1 tablespoon raw sesame seeds
1 tablespoon plus 1 teaspoon Chinese rice wine or dry sherry

UTENSILS

Heavy 12-inch skillet
2 large saucepans
1 medium-size saucepan with cover
2 small saucepans
Vegetable steamer
Ovenproof platter
Small plate

2 large mixing bowls
Small bowl
Small serving bowl
Large strainer
Measuring cups and spoons
Chinese cleaver or chef's knife
Paring knife
Clam or oyster knife
Chinese mesh spoon or long-handled slotted metal spoon
Metal turner
Hand mixer

START-TO-FINISH STEPS

1. Shuck oysters, if using fresh ones, and follow oyster fritter recipe steps 1 through 3.
2. Peel eggplant and follow eggplant recipe step 1.
3. Follow broccoli recipe steps 1 through 3.
4. Follow eggplant recipe steps 2 through 4.
5. Preheat oven to 200 degrees. Follow oyster fritter recipe steps 4 through 6.
6. Follow eggplant recipe steps 5 through 7.
7. To finish, follow broccoli recipe step 5, eggplant recipe step 8, and oyster fritter recipe step 7. Serve.

RECIPES

Five-Fragrance Oyster Fritters

Ginger-soy-vinegar dip:
2 quarter-size slices ginger, peeled and finely chopped
2 tablespoons dark soy sauce
¼ cup Chinese red rice vinegar

16 to 18 large fresh oysters, shucked, or 2 eight-ounce containers shucked oysters, drained
4 eggs
2 tablespoons plus ½ cup peanut or corn oil
⅔ cup all-purpose flour
1½ teaspoons baking powder
1½ teaspoons Chinese five-spice
1 teaspoon salt
¼ teaspoon freshly ground white pepper
3 scallions, white and some green, cut into thin rounds
1 head Boston or Bibb lettuce for garnish (optional)

1. Bring 4 cups water to a rolling boil in large saucepan.
2. Combine ingredients for dip in small serving bowl.
3. Add oysters to the boiling water and remove from heat. Pour oysters into strainer and immerse in bowl of cold water. Drain and pat dry with paper towels. Set aside.
4. In large mixing bowl, beat eggs with 2 tablespoons of the peanut or corn oil until foamy. Add dry ingredients. Beat until smooth. Stir in scallions and oysters.
5. Heat heavy skillet over moderate heat and add ⅓ cup of remaining oil. When oil is hot but not smoking, spoon 2 to 3 tablespoons of batter with 1 or 2 oysters into the skillet: there should be room for 3 to 4 fritters.
6. Cook, turning them, until both sides are golden brown.

Keep warm in oven while you finish cooking remaining oyster-batter mixture. Add more oil as needed.
7. Serve hot on a bed of lettuce, if desired, with ginger-soy-vinegar dip.

Steamed Sesame Eggplant

1 eggplant (about 1 pound), peeled
1 tablespoon raw sesame seeds
3 tablespoons *hoisin* sauce
1 tablespoon dark soy sauce
1 teaspoon Chinese rice wine or dry sherry
3 scallions
2 tablespoons peanut or corn oil
1 teaspoon sesame oil

1. Cut eggplant into strips 4 inches long and ½ inch thick.
2. Bring 1 inch of water to a boil in medium-size saucepan for steaming. Place eggplant on vegetable steamer, cover, and steam over medium-high heat for 3 to 5 minutes, or until eggplant is soft. Turn off heat and leave cover on.
3. Heat small saucepan over moderate heat. Add sesame seeds and stir constantly with wooden spoon. When they turn golden brown, remove from heat and transfer to small plate to cool. Wipe out pan.
4. Combine *hoisin* sauce, soy sauce, and wine or sherry in small bowl. Set aside.
5. Trim scallions, leaving some of the green tops, and cut into 1½-inch lengths. Shred each piece lengthwise.
6. Heat peanut or corn oil in the small saucepan. When oil is hot, add two thirds of the shredded scallions. Stir and cook several seconds, or until scallions soften.
7. Add *hoisin* mixture and stir over medium to high heat. When sauce bubbles, turn off heat. Add sesame oil.
8. Remove eggplant to serving bowl and pour sauce over. Top with toasted sesame seeds and remaining scallion.

Jade-Green Broccoli

4 tablespoons peanut or corn oil
1 small bunch broccoli
2 tablespoons oyster sauce
1 tablespoon dark soy sauce
1 teaspoon sesame oil
1 tablespoon Chinese rice wine or dry sherry

1. Bring 2 quarts water to a boil in large saucepan for blanching broccoli. Add 2 tablespoons of the peanut or corn oil.
2. Wash broccoli and discard tough leaves. Cut flower parts into finger-size pieces. Peel tough skins from stems and cut stems diagonally into thin slices. Set aside.
3. Combine remaining peanut or corn oil, oyster sauce, soy sauce, sesame oil, and wine or sherry in small saucepan. Set aside.
4. Blanch broccoli in the boiling water 1 minute, then remove with Chinese mesh spoon or slotted metal spoon. Shake off excess water and place on serving platter.
5. Heat oyster sauce mixture over moderate heat. When sauce begins to bubble, remove from heat and pour over broccoli.

Pork Shreds and Szechwan Pickle Soup
Beef and Scallops with Oyster Sauce
Stir-Fried Snow Peas with Mushrooms and Almonds / Rice

Varied in color, flavor, and texture, the beef with scallops, stir-fried snow peas with miniature ears of corn, and shredded pork and pickle soup make a pleasing display against bamboo or wood.

The Chinese do not eat as much beef as Westerners do and do not raise beef cattle. Instead, their beef comes from water buffalo or oxen, long past their prime, so that the meat is tough and strong-tasting. Cantonese chefs rarely serve anything resembling a steak but shred, mince, or slice their beef, often marinating it to make the meat palatable, then tossing it together with a variety of other ingredients, such as the scallops and oyster sauce in this recipe.

The Szechwan pickle in the soup is not at all like the Western-style preserved cucumber. Instead, it is a hot, spiced preserved mustard green root with a unique flavor. There are no Western substitutes, but the pickle is readily sold in Chinese markets, either loose in a crock or in cans.

WHAT TO DRINK

Try a full-bodied, dry white wine with the full flavors here: an inexpensive California Chardonnay or, even better, a fully dry Sauvignon Blanc; a white Burgundy from Mâcon or an inexpensive Chablis; an Italian Greco di Tufo or a fully dry Orvieto.

SHOPPING LIST AND STAPLES

1 pound flank steak
4 ounces lean pork cutlet or boned pork chop
½ pound sea or bay scallops
½ pound snow peas
1 large bunch scallions
1 small red bell pepper
Fresh ginger
2 medium-size cloves garlic
2-inch chunk Szechwan pickle
15-ounce can Chinese baby corn
15-ounce can Chinese straw mushrooms
¼ cup plus 2 teaspoons oyster sauce
8-ounce can water chestnuts
4 cups unsalted Chinese Chicken Stock (see page 13)
2⅓ cups peanut or corn oil
4 teaspoons Oriental sesame oil
2 tablespoons dark soy sauce
1 teaspoon light soy sauce
1 cup uncooked rice
2 tablespoons plus 4 teaspoons cornstarch
1¼ teaspoons sugar
Salt
¼ cup sliced almonds
4 tablespoons plus 2 teaspoons Chinese rice wine or dry
  sherry

UTENSILS

Wok
  or Dutch oven (for beef)
  and heavy 12-inch skillet (for snow peas)
Large saucepan
2 medium-size saucepans with covers (1 for rice)
3 medium-size plates
Small plate
Large mixing bowl
Medium-size bowl
4 small bowls
Metal colander
Measuring cups and spoon
Chinese cleaver or chef's knife
Paring knife
Chinese mesh spoon or long-handled slotted metal spoon
16-inch chopsticks or 2 long-handled wooden spoons

START-TO-FINISH STEPS

1. Prepare Szechwan pickle for soup, step 1.
2. Follow general rice recipe on page 12, steps 1 and 2.
3. Follow beef with scallops recipe steps 1 through 5.
4. Follow pork soup step 2.
5. Prepare snow peas, drain and halve water chestnuts, and follow stir-fried snow peas recipe steps 1 through 4.
6. Bring soup stock to a simmer, step 3.
7. Follow beef with scallops recipe steps 6 through 9.
8. Preheat oven to 200 degrees. Follow pork soup recipe step 4.
9. Complete beef with scallops recipe steps 10 and 11. Follow general rice recipe step 3.
10. Wipe out pan. Cook stir-fried snow peas recipe steps 5 and 6.
11. Follow pork soup recipe step 5. Remove platters of beef with scallops and stir-fried snow peas from oven. Serve with rice.

RECIPES

Pork Shreds and Szechwan Pickle Soup

2-inch chunk Szechwan pickle
4 ounces lean pork cutlet or boned pork chop
2 teaspoons cornstarch
1 teaspoon light soy sauce
1 teaspoon sesame oil
4 cups unsalted Chinese Chicken Stock
1 scallion

1. Thoroughly wash pickle in warm water to rinse off all spices. Cut it into thin shreds and soak in small bowl with 4 cups water about 20 minutes. Rinse and drain.
2. Cut pork cutlets into thin shreds to make about ½ cup. In small bowl combine cornstarch, soy sauce, and sesame oil. Add the shredded pork and toss well.
3. In medium-size saucepan, bring chicken stock and soaked pickle to a simmer, and cover.
4. Wash and trim scallion, leaving some of green top. Cut into thin rounds.
5. Add pork mixture to the simmering stock, separating the pieces with chopsticks or a fork. Simmer about 20 seconds, or until pork shreds are no longer pink. Add scallion and salt to taste. Serve hot.

Beef and Scallops with Oyster Sauce

1 tablespoon dark soy sauce
2 teaspoons sesame oil
2 tablespoons plus 2 teaspoons cornstarch
1 teaspoon sugar
1 pound flank steak
½ pound sea or bay scallops
3 tablespoons plus 2 teaspoons Chinese rice wine or dry sherry
¼ cup oyster sauce
2 tablespoons water
4 scallions
1 quarter-size slice fresh ginger, peeled and minced
2 medium-size cloves garlic, minced
1 small red bell pepper, seeds and ribs removed, cut into thin strips
6 ears baby corn, rinsed and cut in half lengthwise
6 water chestnuts, rinsed and cut in half
2 cups peanut or corn oil

1. Combine soy sauce, sesame oil, 2 tablespoons of the cornstarch, and ¼ teaspoon of the sugar in large mixing bowl and stir well.

2. Using cleaver or knife held at an angle, cut flank steak on the diagonal (against fiber) into pieces ⅛ inch thick and 2 inches long. Add to soy marinade and toss, making sure to coat all the beef slices. Set aside.

3. In small bowl, combine oyster sauce with remaining ¾ teaspoon sugar, Chinese rice wine, and water, and set aside.

4. Wash and trim scallions, leaving some of green tops. Cut in half lengthwise and then into ½-inch pieces. Place ginger, garlic, pepper, baby corn, and water chestnuts in separate piles on medium-sized plate.

5. If using sea scallops, cut them in half. Leave bay scallops whole. Put scallops in medium-size bowl. Add remaining 2 teaspoons of cornstarch. Toss gently to mix well.

6. Heat wok or Dutch oven over high heat and add peanut or corn oil. When oil is very hot but not smoking—a good test is to see whether a small piece of scallion sizzles when dropped in—add beef mixture and gently separate pieces with chopsticks or with 2 long-handled wooden spoons. Cook beef over high heat about 1 minute, or until beef just loses its redness. Remove with Chinese mesh spoon or long-handled slotted metal spoon and shake off any excess oil. Turn onto another medium-sized plate lined with paper towels to drain further.

7. Turn heat to low and add scallops. Cook about 30 seconds. Remove scallops with Chinese mesh spoon or slotted metal spoon to the plate with the beef.

8. Pour off all but 2 tablespoons of oil from the wok or Dutch oven. (You may strain and save the oil for cooking other Chinese dishes.) Turn heat to high and heat oil until it is very hot. Add scallions, ginger, and garlic. When garlic turns golden, about 2 seconds, add red pepper, baby corn, and water chestnuts. Stir about 10 seconds, or until just heated through.

9. Add oyster sauce mixture and stir until it bubbles.

10. Return beef and scallops (along with any juices that have accumulated on plate) to pan. Stir several seconds to reheat.

11. Immediately remove food to heatproof platter. Cover with foil and keep warm in oven.

Stir-Fried Snow Peas with Mushrooms and Almonds

½ pound snow peas, washed and strings removed
6 ears baby corn, cut in half lengthwise
⅓ cup Chinese straw mushrooms
6 water chestnuts, drained and halved
¼ teaspoon salt
¼ teaspoon sugar
1 tablespoon dark soy sauce
2 teaspoons oyster sauce
1 tablespoon Chinese rice wine or pale dry sherry
1 tablespoon water
1 teaspoon sesame oil
⅓ cup peanut or corn oil
¼ cup sliced almonds
1 scallion

1. Bring 6 cups water to a boil in large saucepan.

2. Add snow peas, baby corn, straw mushrooms, and water chestnuts. Immediately pour them into metal colander and rinse under cold water to stop the cooking. Drain and set aside on medium-sized plate.

3. In small mixing bowl, combine soy sauce, oyster sauce, water, wine or sherry, sesame oil, sugar, and salt. Stir well and set aside.

4. Trim scallion, leaving some of green top. Cut in half lengthwise and then into 1½-inch pieces. Set aside on small plate.

5. Heat wok or heavy skillet over moderate heat. Add peanut or corn oil. When oil is hot, add almonds and cook, stirring about 30 seconds, until golden brown. Turn off heat and remove almonds with Chinese mesh spoon or slotted metal spoon to drain on paper towels.

6. Pour off all but 2 tablespoons of oil from the pan. Turn heat to high. When oil is hot, add chopped scallion and cook 3 to 4 seconds. Add blanched snow peas, baby corn, straw mushrooms, and water chestnuts. Stir fry about 20 seconds to reheat. Stir and swirl in oyster sauce mixture. Stir several seconds, then transfer to serving platter. Top with the toasted almonds and keep warm in oven.

ADDED TOUCH

Fresh fruit is always welcome after a Chinese meal. Try this simple orange dessert:

1. Peel 3 chilled oranges and cut crosswise into thin slices.

2. Remove seeds and divide slices into equal portions on serving plates.

3. Sprinkle small amount of sweetened coconut flakes and chopped crystallized ginger on top.

4. Garnish with fresh mint, if available.

Acknowledgments

The Editors with to thank the following for their contributions to the conception and production of these books: Ezra Bowen, Judith Brennan, Angelica Cannon, Elizabeth Schneider Colchie, Marion Flynn, Freida Henry, Jay Jacobs, Pearl Lau, Kay Noble, Elizabeth Noll, Fran Shinagel, Martha Tippin, Ann Topper, Jack Ubaldi.

The Editors would also like to thank the following for their courtesy in lending items for photography: Arabia of Finland; Balos Giftware; Georges Briard Designs, Inc.; Brunschwig and Fils; Buffalo China, Inc.; Caloric; Commercial Aluminum Cookware Company; Copco; Country Floors, Inc.; Fabrications; Peter Fasano Hand-Painted Fabrics; Fitz and Floyd; F.O. Merz–New York; Formica Corporation; Richard Ginori; Ingrid Ltd.; The Lauffer Company; Laura Ashley; Leacock and Company; Mosseri Industries; Mottahedeh and Company, Inc.; Patino-Wolf Associates; Pottery Barn; Robot-Coupe International; Royal Copenhagen Porcelain; Sturbridge Village; Wallace Silversmiths; White-Westinghouse; Williams-Sonoma. Special thanks to: Broadway Panhandler; Barbara Eigen Pottery; Far Eastern Antiques; Pierre Deux; and Reed & Barton Silversmiths.

Illustrations by Ray Skibinski.

Ordering Special Ingredients by Mail

Although most supermarkets stock at least some basic ingredients for Chinese cooking, you may want to locate other possibly more complete sources near you. There are various ways to track down suppliers of Chinese ingredients: check the yellow pages of your phone directory for listings of Chinese grocers, Chinese restaurants, Chinese organizations, or Chinese shops. Where there is an Oriental community of any size, you should be able to locate a source of ingredients, both canned and fresh. Also, check local specialty food shops or health food stores; these often carry Oriental food products. As a last resort, you can mail order Chinese ingredients from one of the sources listed below. Some also sell utensils. Before ordering, contact each supplier to ask for a catalog and price list, or contact the Organization of Chinese Americans, a group that has twenty-seven chapters located in twenty-two different states. Their address is: Organization of Chinese Americans, Inc., 2025 I Street, NW, Suite 926, Washington, DC 20006. Their phone number is: (202) 223-5500.

The West Coast
Orient Delight Market, 865 East El Camino Real, Mountain View, CA 94040; (415) 969–4288

The Midwest
Woks 'N' Things, 2234 S. Wentworth Ave., Chicago, IL 60616; (312) 842–0701

The Southwest
Jung's Oriental Food, 2519 N. Fitzhugh, Dallas, TX 75204; (214) 827–7653

The East
Wok Talk, 420 Lexington Ave., Suite 2626, New York, NY 10170; (212) 986–1034
Chinese Kitchen, PO Box 218, Dept. T, Sterling, NJ 07980; (201) 665–2234

Index

Time-Life Books Inc. offers a wide range of fine recordings, including a Big Band series. For subscription information, call 1-800-621-7026, or write TIME-LIFE MUSIC, Time & Life Building, Chicago, Illinois 60611.